THIS WAS OUR CITY
Tim Keogh

This is a book about "failure" — hope you enjoy it!

Tim

keoboy

Copyright © 2013 by Tim Keogh.

All rights reserved. No part of this publication may be reproduced, stored in a retrieval system, or transmitted in any form without the prior written consent of the author.

Published by Keoboy Publications.

Email. keoboy@fsmail.net

Printed and bound by Deanprint, Stockport, Cheshire.

Cover by Michael Bradbury.

Cover photo by Shirley Baker © Mary Evans Picture Library.

City photo © The Manchester Evening News.

Author photos © Tim Keogh.

ISBN: 978-0-9562881-1-0.

In memory of Irene Keogh (1927-1997).

Contents.

1. God Save The Queen.   7.
2. Back to the Futchers.   17.
3. A Winter of Discontent.   27.
4. London Calling.   37.
5. The Smith's Arms.   49.
6. Pale Blues.   63.
7. Terrace apart, again.   77.
8. First Class.   93.
9. Strange Fruit.   111.
10. Fine Times.   121.
11. The Changing of the Guard.   129.

Ian Brightwell fights for the ball in front of the Kippax against Q.P.R. in September 1986.

ONE.

GOD SAVE THE QUEEN.

"Come back you lanky get! I want to stab you!"
The words pierced the chill North Manchester midnight air. I did not hang around to check as to whether the spotty youth chasing me was actually carrying a knife. Instead the absurd thought flashed through my mind that I had never run as well as this on school sports day. I tore across the concrete wasteland known to previous generations as the Central Gardens up the hill past the Dusty Miller public house and crouched down behind a low wall, my heart beating like a blacksmith's hammer. The pounding footsteps seemed to have stopped. As my mind raced I tried to gather my thoughts. Directly behind me was the bowling green where my beloved grandad would be engaging in a combat of his own in a few hours time. He would be horrified if he knew I was in this situation. The only sounds that I could hear were the whirring of the fork lift trucks and the distant voices of the night shift delivery staff at the nearby shopping centre. I hope that Macker had got away. There were three or four chasing him. Ambushed in Tommy's chippy! Our only crime was the fact that we had attended the local Grammar School. It must have been the way we ordered our chips. Realising that the sword was far mightier than the pen we ran for it. Twenty minutes passed. It seemed like hours. The coast was finally clear. Macker had not been so lucky. No thanks to the fashionable faux pas of wearing clogs that summer he was slower off the mark than me, tripped, fell full length and was given a good kicking behind the Post Office.

It was the Summer of 1977. The Queen's Silver Jubilee. The Sex Pistols had declared that there was "Anarchy in the U.K." Bands were coming out of the woodwork all across Manchester like The Buzzcocks, Slaughter and the Dogs, The Fall and Warsaw. In a flat on the Hollins estate in Middleton guitarist Dave Fielding nodded in recognition of the childhood scrapes we shared along the Boarshaw Road. I looked on across the chasm of a room as Mark Burgess was putting together The Chameleons who would soon be shifting albums by the bucket load. It had been fourteen years since the Beatles had played in Middleton and now it was the turn of The Damned, The Jam and The Boomtown Rats to play concerts at the newly opened Civic Hall. Looking at the punks with their Mohican hairstyles and Vivienne Westwood inspired safety pins and bondage gear I secretly envied their style and individuality. But I sensed intuitively that I was hardly a punk rocker in the making, and that I would be destined to be on the outside looking in. The atmosphere was electric on these particular nights. It all kicked off after The Boomtown Rats' concert leaving a boy fighting for his life in the street. The Middleton Guardian reported that Bob Geldof and fellow members of his band accompanied the young fan to hospital, thus recognising Geldof's heroic nature some eight years before the rest of the world caught on!

Macker had not been seen since the ambush at the chip shop but nothing would stop the two of us supporting our beloved Manchester City. There he was at the end of Kingsway at the usual time of one thirty waiting for the orange and white SELNEC bus to appear on the horizon. While we waited we impatiently flicked through our brand new Kippax Street season ticket books and scanned our foldaway fixture cards which were given away by the Football Pink at the start of every season. Few words were spoken between the two of us. We took up our places on the salmon pink vandal proof seats on the top deck of the bus and tried not to look anybody in the eye as the number seventeen went through the lights at Victoria Avenue down past Blackley fire station and up the hill past Boggart Hole Clough. The journey seemed to take longer than usual as we eyed every small group of young men with suspicion. Nobody was wearing any scarves today and we did not know who was red or who was blue. Moston Lane, Harpurhey and

Collyhurst were negotiated safely before the bus emptied us reluctantly at Shudehill and we scurried off in the direction of Piccadilly. Where were the Saturday shoppers? We took some consolation in the fact that there were police officers on every corner and we never stopped to question why we were putting ourselves through this strange dangerous ritual. We caught the 76X Match Bus on Aytoun Street across from the derelict Grand Hotel and sat as near to the driver downstairs as we could. Our progress was halted as we hit heavy traffic as the bus inched along the back of the University and I got my first glimpse of the floodlights above the rooftops ahead. The sight of floodlights never failed to move me especially on an away trip to an unfamiliar ground. It was then that I noticed a massive group of Cockney Reds marching along to our left, marshalled on all sides by the grim faced local constabulary and their even grimmer salivating police dogs.

" We're gonna win the Football League this year" came the chant from the back of the Kippax as the last strains of "The Boys in Blue" faded into the background. We stood in our usual place about twelve steps up from the front bang on the halfway line to the left of Big Ted and his crowd of bus drivers from the nearby depot. Today felt different to a regular home game. There was great tension around the stadium. The segregated United fans to our left on the Kippax were in full voice and there was a constant procession of fans being "escorted" from the ground in headlocks or with their arms twisted agonisingly up their backs by the bobbies who although somewhat red faced seemed to be relishing the challenge.

Runners up in May to champions Liverpool, City had a fine side which I genuinely thought had a great chance of actually winning the League and taking over as the number one team in Manchester. In goal was the great Joe Corrigan who was constantly fighting it out with Ray Clemence and Peter Shilton to be the England number one. At full back there were Kenny Clements and Willie Donachie, with two from three from Mike Doyle,

Tommy Booth and Dave Watson in the centre. Asa Hartford commanded the midfield ably assisted by either Gary Owen or Paul Power. Years ahead of its time, on the wings the left footed Peter Barnes cut in from the right and the right footed Dennis Tueart cut in from the left. Up front Brian Kidd was partnered by either Joe Royle or new signing Mick Channon. The great Colin Bell despite a brief reappearance in April 1976 was still engaged in his long battle back to full fitness after his devastating injury against the Reds in November 1975.

United were now managed by Dave Sexton who had recently undergone a tricky charisma by-pass. Nevertheless he had assembled a fine attacking side which included Stuart Pearson, Lou Macari, Steve Coppell and Gordon Hill. But it was City who flew at the United defence from the kick off and who took the lead just before the quarter hour with a free kick from Brian Kidd that nearly burst the net at the Platt Lane End. The crowd surged forward and for a few seconds there was mayhem as we hugged total strangers whilst struggling to keep our feet. Joe Corrigan saved everything that was thrown at him as United tried to get back in the game but a second goal from Kiddo early in the second half announced to one and all that this was our day. All the tension of the build up disappeared to be replaced by absolute elation. Asa Hartford crossed, Channon shot and it was three nil to the Blues! "I never felt more like singing the blues, City win, United lose...." The Kippax erupted in a sea of blue and white. Jimmy Nicholl scored a late consolation for United giving City a victory by three goals to one and the local bragging rights until the next time. Local boy Brian Kidd captured all the headlines the next day. We left the ground on cloud nine and sang our way back to the Parkside and the Match bus home with scarcely a thought about any trouble. The United fans were long gone in their attempts to catch their trains and coaches back home to Dublin, Dundee and Humberside.

I had just started work as an office boy in a bank in Manchester city centre. I was no punk rocker! Who was I kidding? Uncomfortably clad in a three piece suit and huge kipper tie I arrived outside the bank with minutes to spare. I could not bring myself to enter. My stomach was in knots. I walked around the block three times. I would have given anything to have got back on the bus to Middleton. But something eventually persuaded me to ring the bell. I found myself working on the first floor, as an office boy in a room with seven or eight women! Having no sisters, being from a boy's grammar school, hardly having been kissed and blushing bright red at the first sight of a girl, here I was surrounded by a roomful of real women! There was blowsy blonde Pat who was a dead ringer for Bette Lynch off "Coronation Street", "constable" Bev whose look alone could cut you stone dead, and sophisticated smouldering Barbara from Sale who would rather have died than venture into North Manchester. I soon learned that I had to be quick with the repartee as the girls tried to embarrass me with their crude jokes and double meanings. The actual work was mind numbingly boring. I was given the task of sorting out yellow slips from pink slips to a background of the incessant hum of a typewriter and shrill inane greeting of the switchboard operator. All my years of studying had come to this! Fortunately there was some respite. As eleven o'clock approached I was sent around Manchester to deliver messages and buy butties. I would wander into HMV Records on Market Street where I would check out the new releases by bands such as The Buzzcocks, The Stranglers, The Jam, Eddie and The Hot Rods and the Salford punk poet John Cooper Clarke. In the afternoons I would get the chance to work on the only computer in the office. It was the size of a grand piano and did not have a screen or a mouse.

I was fascinated by the huge bank vaults, the sheer volume of keys, the antiquated furniture and the archaic ways of doing things. People were still using fountain pens, calligraphy, and huge dusty ledgers to document everything. It was a throwback to Charles Dickens and every morning I would glance around to see if Bob Cratchit had arrived. Apart from the bevy of beauties on the first floor I soon gravitated downstairs to the real characters in the office, Frank and Wilf, who were the two bank "guards" or "messengers". Wilf would greet me cheerily every morning clad in his bank uniform before setting out on his rounds around town delivering important letters. I was thrilled to accompany him as he stopped for a chat and a brew in every nook and cranny in the giant offices and banks in the King Street area of the city. He reminded me very much of Fletcher, the old lag from "Porridge", and I was proud to be his Godber. I hung on his every word as we spent whole mornings and afternoons strolling through the labyrinth of streets in the financial district. The term Bank Guard could not really apply to Frank. With all due respect, he would not have been able to guard a cup of tea, let alone the Manchester Liners sub branch out at the docks which was entrusted to him. He was in his late seventies, no more than four feet tall, and as deaf as a post. He was utterly charming and I looked forward to seeing him every day. He told me about his youth and how he used to ride his motor bike at top speed to impress the ladies just after the First World War! He rarely answered the question that you asked him but I did not mind. I do not know how I kept my face straight when one particularly hot summers day his hair appeared to melt and run down his face. "Boot polish" advised Wilf out of the corner of his mouth.

The Blues were making heavy weather of the autumn fixture list. New signing Mick Channon had already succumbed to injury which did not bode well for the future. He missed a draw at Everton, a heavy defeat at Coventry and a hard fought home victory against Arsenal. On the 29th of October the great Liverpool side with new signing Kenny Dalglish and a very young Alan Hansen in their ranks arrived at Maine Road confident of a victory against a City side without stars Hartford and Tueart. But on this cold dismal autumnal afternoon inspired largely by a brilliant display from young Peter Barnes the Blues simply tore them apart by three goals to one. The official attendance was 49207 but it seemed much more, so tightly were we packed on the Kippax. The first goal was put in from close range by Brian Kidd after Channon had flicked on a Barnes corner. The second was finished by Mick Channon from a Watson through ball. His Cheshire cat grin and whirling arm let us all know that he had enjoyed scoring his fourth goal of the season. But the roof came off the Kippax as Peter Barnes ran right through the centre of the famous Liverpool defence bypassing the hapless Hansen before passing to Joe Royle who smashed the ball past Ray Clemence. This was to be the last act of Joe's playing career at City. It seemed strange at the time and even stranger now that he was allowed to go to Bristol City where he sensationally scored four on his debut. First team squads were small and City were getting through a season using only fifteen or sixteen players in those days. A couple of injuries to attackers would have left them really stretched. Yet manager Tony Book took the decision to let the popular striker go.

Liverpool were not the only high profile visitors to Manchester that autumn. The Stranglers had moved from venues such as the Electric Circus in Collyhurst where I had watched them only a few short months ago and were due to play at The Apollo at Ardwick Green. The Apollo was now re-establishing itself as the premier concert venue in Manchester. The girls at work were less than impressed when I showed them the cover of the latest Stranglers LP "Rattus Norvegicus" with its huge picture of a giant rodent. And when I told them that there was a possibility that live rats would be released from a bucket into the audience from the stage they made their feelings very clear. There were fears expressed in the press that the "degenerate" punks would tear up the first few rows of seats as the band made their entrance.

"But I have got front row seats for Diana Ross on Saturday" complained the subdued typist Joan in a rare display of emotion. She need not have worried. The live rats, too, did not make an appearance but the music was electric as the band pumped out favourites like "Get a grip", "Peaches" and new single "No More Heroes". As I looked around in awe at the spit drenched pogoing crowd I thought of another day at the bank sorting out the pink slips from the yellow. Something had better change.

City were still struggling to find consistency as Christmas approached, knocked out of the UEFA Cup at the first attempt by a little known Polish side Widzew Lodz on away goals. As City carelessly threw away a two goal lead in the first leg a wag on the Kippax was heard to shout "What is wrong Widzew Lads?" We all needed a real lift from somewhere and it came on Boxing Day with Newcastle United the visitors. Unbeknown to us and to many in the tightly packed crowd this game was to take on huge significance in the folklore of the club as the afternoon unfolded. The first half ended goalless as Macker removed his customary tangerine from his pocket for his half time snack. This always raised a laugh from mate Phil and I. Most others around us were smoking Players Number 6 or retiring to the ramshackle bars at the back of the stand for a couple of swiftly necked Harp Lagers. But for Macker it was always a tangerine or even a carrot! From our central position near the front of the Kippax we could see right down the tunnel and watch the emergence of the players a few precious seconds before the majority of the crowd. It was clear on this day that something momentous was happening. There was a real buzz which seemed to be spreading through the crowd in the Main Stand opposite us. There amongst the players gently limbering up was the great Colin Bell. He had spent the last eighteen months battling heroically against the terrible injury that he suffered in the Manchester derby back in November 1975. Nobody really thought that they would ever see him play again. And yet here he was wearing the famous Sky Blue shirt. I could not speak. There were no words that could do justice to what I was witnessing. People were applauding, cheering and crying. I cannot recall just how long this wall of sound went on for. It seemed endless. The atmosphere in the ground was quite unreal especially coming as it did after such a boring first half. The team itself was galvanised. Newcastle were taken apart. The goals rained in. Three by Tueart and one by Kidd. The score did not seem to matter. Colin Bell was back.

The season was suddenly up and running again. It seemed that the sheer presence of Colin the King in his old number 8 shirt was giving new life to those around him. It was true that Colin did not have the full mobility in his injured knee and there was I am sad to say a pronounced limp as he moved around the pitch. But to us this did not matter. We were thrilled to have him back and had great faith that he would fully recover. All around him players were transformed. Gary Owen in particular seemed to spring into life as he scored three goals in the next five games. The Blues won seven league games in a row and began to move up the table in a bid to hang on to the shirt tails of leaders Nottingham Forest who were riding high under their great manager Brian Clough.

Clough and his assistant Peter Taylor had assembled a magnificent underrated side which included Peter Shilton in goal, Larry Lloyd and Kenny Burns at the back who resembled extras from a spaghetti western, John McGovern, Archie Gemmill and Ian Bowyer in midfield, the wily John Robertson on the wing, with Gary Birtles and Tony Woodcock up front. At the end of January City were drawn against Forest in the F.A. Cup. I made the trip down to the Midlands two times in four days only to see the Blues suffer a narrow defeat. The game was postponed due to fog on the Saturday which we only discovered on the primitive car radio in a pub car park on the outskirts of Nottingham after a perilous five hour journey down the M1. Undaunted, I repeated the trip the following Tuesday for the rearranged game, narrowly avoiding being thrown into the Trent by the Forest fans who lay in wait along the river, only for the Blues to go down by two goals to one in a closely fought encounter.

All of a sudden the season came to a shuddering halt. Out of Europe and now out of the Cup. And then the bombshell! Dennis Tueart was deemed to be surplus to requirements! I was completely devastated. As far as I was concerned Dennis was our most dangerous player. How could they think of selling him? Perhaps he made unreasonable demands to the club which Tony Book felt unable to grant? In those internet free days with no Sky Sports News club business was kept under wraps. I think that allowing Tueart to leave must rank, along with the earlier decision of letting Francis Lee go to Derby, as one of the poorest decisions that the club ever made. In my view City that year were little short of being a championship winning side. Consequently we won only three of the remaining thirteen league fixtures losing heavily at both Highbury and Anfield. Nevertheless the Blues still managed a highly creditable fourth place in the league scoring a fantastic 74 goals in the process. Brian Kidd top scored with 16 goals followed by Channon and Tueart who scored twelve apiece. In June after 551 appearances Mike Doyle was transferred to Stoke City for £50000. He had been a truly great servant to the club winning League, F.A.Cup, League Cup, and European Cup Winners Cup medals. He also played five times for England towards the end of his City career. It really felt like it was the end of an era, but I had absolute blind faith in the fact that City must know what they were doing and that such decisions were always made for the good of the club.

TWO.

BACK TO THE FUTCHERS.

"Maine Road, please." I demanded as I sat down in the back of the black cab in St. Ann's Square on that sunny summer afternoon in 1978. As the taxi wove its way through the busy city centre streets I nervously glanced at my watch and wondered if I would be able to get there and back in the hour that I had for my lunch. I desperately needed to get my ticket before the new season got underway at the weekend. I smoothed down the creases of my new suit trousers and adjusted my tie as the cab pulled up on the forecourt of Maine Road, the home of Manchester City.

"Can you please wait for me? I should only be fifteen minutes or so." I enquired as I looked across at the small boy kicking his ball at the wall outside the main entrance.

"O.K. guy," replied the cabbie as he wound his window down and took out a packet of Players from his breast pocket. As I scampered away in the direction of the Ticket Office on the corner by the North Stand I was thrilled to see practically the whole First Team Squad emerge from the ground and make for their cars. I was only yards away from them and my eyes met those of Brian Kidd who to my complete astonishment greeted me cheerily and walked over to ask what I was doing. I could hardly get my words out but managed to somehow convey that I had come down to buy a season ticket for the new season. I was rendered speechless when he walked along with me and actually took me into the offices and asked one of the secretaries if they could "fix me up with a ticket". He then wished me luck and went on his way. A few minutes later I returned to the taxi in a state of high excitement.

"Have you done it, then?" the driver asked.

"Yeah," I replied as I slumped into my seat.

"What position do you play?" he went on as the taxi turned out of Great Western Street in the direction of the city centre.

" ..Er, centre forward, usually...." I stammered as it began to dawn on me that he thought I had just signed for City.

"I thought that you might do. How tall are you? You must be six-two, at least. That was Kiddo you were talking to, you know. You will be after his place, I suppose…" I chuckled to myself, glanced again at my watch and shifted uneasily in my seat.

The summer of 1978 brought Patti Smith into the charts with "Because the Night", The Rolling Stones went disco with "Miss You" and Kate Bush took the number one spot with "Wuthering Heights". I went down to London to see Bob Dylan perform his first concerts in the UK for twelve years. His recent albums "Blood on the tracks" and "Desire" had brought Dylan a whole new generation of fans. One of whom was me. I listened to John Peel long into the night with my transistor radio hidden under the bed clothes hoping to catch a track from the new LP "Street Legal". The concert was to take place at Blackbushe Aerodrome in deepest darkest Surrey. I managed to cadge a lift down to the outskirts of the capital and being so incredibly naïve fully expected to stay in one of the many bed and breakfasts that I imagined thronged the M25! Accompanied by younger brother Pete, we made our way across the city to Waterloo station where "Terry met Julie every Friday night". I did not see Terry or Julie but the station was packed out with "hippies" bound for the concert. I looked around and realised that we were hopelessly unprepared for the weekend. Dressed in cagoule and jeans with not even a bag of crisps to our name we looked on as the hippies loaded their hampers and tents onto the fleet of special trains bound for the concert site. Two hours later after tramping through countless country lanes we found ourselves in a huge field amongst a crowd of biblical proportions. The field was full of tents including Indian teepees, huge bonfires and flags of every nation. Even at this hour there were troubadours and all manner of entertainers. The night air was filled with smoke and the distinct aroma of cannabis. To our right a vast walled city which I presumed was the actual site of the concert. I looked at my watch. A quarter to three. The concert was due to start at midday with Dylan not due on stage for some seventeen hours! It was bloody freezing! I could not feel my toes.

"Hey man! Why not come and crash out in our tent?" said a voice out of the darkness. Way out of my depth but absolutely frozen I had no hesitation in taking up his offer. When my eyes became accustomed to the light I saw that at least fifty sweaty bodies were crammed together like sardines in what was basically a family size tent! I dossed down in the corner and tried to get some sleep.

The crowd were on the move. Bleary eyed and shattered we followed the throng across the field to the festival site. It was only a little after five but the gates were due to open! Like everybody else we ran to take up our places but found ourselves positioned at least a football pitch away from the stage. There was not a single punk in sight. This was a hippies graveyard! I turned down the regular offers of magic mushrooms, fried bananas, and all manner of substances as the day passed in a haze interspersed with music from Eric Clapton and Graham Parker among others. There were huge lorries officially selling sweets and hot beverages but behind the bonbons and lukewarm tea you could unofficially buy a dozen lagers at a time! Helicopters brought in the alumni of the rock world including assorted Stones and Beatle Ringo Starr before Dylan hit the stage dead on time. There were no video screens so the band looked like travelling fleas. But there was no dispute that the music was amazing. Three hours later we were back on the country lanes amongst the crowds inching their way back to the trains to London. A voice from nowhere chimed that he wanted a "White Riot". Nobody had the slightest inclination to do so. We slept on the steps of the Gents toilets back at Waterloo before catching the best thing to come out of London. The train back to Manchester.

New signing Paul Futcher made his debut alongside Dave Watson in the back four as the season opened with a hard earned point at Derby County. He certainly seemed a stylish player with the ball at his feet but to my eyes he was alarmingly slow on the turn. Like a number 59 bus! His brother Ron was recruited as a striker to provide cover for Kidd and Channon. After a sensational start to his City career in which he scored a hat trick at Stamford Bridge in a four-one victory over Chelsea he soon retreated into the shadows. The third signing of the close season was that of veteran Colin Viljoen who had served Ipswich Town so well for many years. His arrival at Maine Road was a clear indication that Colin Bell was again struggling for fitness, and indeed Bell was to make only three League appearances over the next eight months. City had to wait until the fifth game of the season for a victory when they convincingly despatched a poor Leeds United side by three goals to nil.

City had again qualified for the U.E.F.A. Cup by virtue of finishing fourth in the League and as I was now earning money (sixty four pounds a month to be precise) I decided to make plans to go to the first European away game. The draw paired us with the Dutch side Twente Enschede. It goes without saying that I had never heard of them, but when the newly formed Travel Club announced that they would be running trips to nearby Amsterdam I could hardly contain myself. It was one thing to follow City all over the country during these years blighted by hooliganism, but to contemplate a trip to the continent may have been a step too far for my parents. At that time there were regular reports of the mayhem caused in Europe by followers of Leeds, Man United, and of course England. Incredibly mum and dad gave me the green light. But I could not convince any of my immediate City pals to go with me. I had spent the last three or four years travelling the country alone watching the Blues so there was nothing else for it. I had to bite the bullet and go on my own!

City as a club were very conscious of preserving their own good reputation as far as the behaviour of their fans was concerned. The Supporters Club immediately set up a Travel Club which everybody had to join if they intended going on the official club trip. Incredibly the secretary of the local Supporters Club came round to my house one evening and actually interviewed me to assess my suitability towards making the trip! As an ex Grammar School boy working in a bank in Manchester the hard men of Europe had little to fear from me. I waited eagerly for my travel club membership card to arrive and before I knew it the great day arrived and along with several hundred Blues I boarded a ferry bound for the Hook of Holland. The crossing was rough but maybe this was due to the strong lager consumed in vast quantities by the majority of us. The camaraderie of the fans was absolutely fantastic. I guess that there were many like me who were making their first trip abroad following the Blues. We checked in at our hotel and had the whole of the afternoon free in Amsterdam. I held my breath and stared straight ahead as we ventured through the infamous red light district with the ladies in the windows and their minders on the nearby bridges. I was terrified. I had never seen anything like it. It was with great relief that we arrived in a bar sporting the Rolling Stones logo on the Leidesplein just off Dam square. The bar was soon filled with City supporters with flags and banners which were soon attached to the walls and the singing began:

"We'll drink, a drink, a drink to Colin the king, the king, the king ….." I found it amazing that you could order drinks and build up a tab paying at the end like the locals. I think some fans did the proverbial runner but not me! I did not fancy spending the evening in an Amsterdam police station. The afternoon wore on in a blue haze. Fantastic!

As the coaches pulled up outside the ground at Enschede a tremendous sight awaited us. The local townspeople all came out of their houses and applauded us! Imagine that happening at Anfield or Elland Road. Youngsters approached us offering to swap badges and scarves. In fact I still possess a Twente Enschede silk red and white scarf to this day. The welcome was overwhelming and made me ashamed of some of the antics around First Division grounds on match days back home. We all giggled unkindly as an overweight Blue had great difficulty getting through the turnstile! I bought a match programme but was disappointed to find that it was completely in Dutch apart from a short paragraph offering us a "pleasant and memorable stay". The City team picture revealed several late 70s unflattering haircuts of the mullet variety and a smattering of moustaches. The team had three enforced changes. Paul Power replaced Willie Donachie at left back with Colin Viljoen making his debut in midfield, and Roger Palmer coming in for Brian Kidd up front. FC Twente included a young Frans Thijssen who along with Arnold Muhren were among the first foreign imports into the First Division and both players became star performers for Ipswich Town for a number of years. The City fans were allocated a section of terracing near the corner flag and although the afternoon's beer was beginning to take its toll I was so thrilled to be watching the Blues in Europe. Twente gave a good account of themselves but our midfield was superbly marshalled by Asa Hartford. Dave Watson scored from a corner at our end of the ground and everybody was pretty pleased with a one all draw and was pretty confident of victory in the second leg in a fortnight.

Colin Bell made a rare appearance as substitute as City narrowly overcame the Dutch in the second leg. It was clear from the Kippax that the King was really struggling to get around the pitch and that his limp seemed quite pronounced. A great victory in the next leg over the Belgian side Standard Liege masked the fact that City were having a hard time of it in the League and beginning to slip down the table. Three defeats and a draw in November revealed that goals were suddenly becoming hard to find. Gary Owen was top scorer with six for the season with the prolific Kidd and Channon struggling to find the net. It was then that the U.E.F.A. Cup draw paired City with the great A.C. Milan in Round 3.

City flew out to Milan on the 22nd of November only to find that the match was postponed shortly before kick-off due to swirling fog. Unusually the game was hastily rescheduled for the next afternoon. Manager Tony Book felt that this gave the Blues a psychological edge as the atmosphere was nothing like as intense on a bright crisp winter afternoon. It seems strange nowadays when even pre-season friendlies are televised live but in 1978 we had to rely on the radio for coverage of the game. At work we placed a radio in the gents toilets and I must confess that I had a bad case of the runs that particular day! Let's just say that the seat was occupied for at least ninety minutes. City themselves were quick out of the traps and raced into a two goal lead through Brian Kidd and a sensational solo effort from Paul Power which we were able to catch on the news later that night. Unfortunately Milan hit back straight away and heartbreakingly equalised leaving City only eight minutes away from being the first British club to win in the San Siro Stadium. Still we had to be pleased with a 2-2 draw that set up the second leg perfectly.

I could not sleep for several nights leading up to the game which was to take place on Wednesday December 6th. It did not come much bigger than A.C. Milan at home in a major European competition. I could not concentrate at all in work and watched the minutes slowly tick by on the huge clock opposite my desk. At half past four I rushed out the huge front door, bought an Evening News from Wilf who moonlighted as a paper seller for parts of the afternoon and scurried up Old Bank Street past the Barnaby Rudge restaurant. I scampered up Newmarket, along Norfolk Street past the old Stock Exchange, around the corner past the John Bull pub and the Post Office before arriving breathlessly outside the Trafalgar pub on York Street where I was to meet Macker. The street lights were on and the rain was beginning to fall as I stepped inside the doorway.

"Great news" announced Macker, clad in his trademark grey jumper, as he handed me my pint.

"Channon and Barnes are both fit!" I am not sure how he obtained this information but it proved to be correct. It was also great to see Tommy Booth established in the side once again alongside Dave Watson at the heart of the City defence. The rain had miraculously stopped as we took up our places in the centre of the Kippax. As on all the big nights it seemed more crowded than usual. In fact Macker had a hard job removing his half time tangerine from his pocket. I bought a programme which was full of great colour photos from the first leg, and also informed me that the Souvenir shop had a whole range of Club souvenirs ranging in price from 5p(!) to £15, that I could get a business lunch for £2-20 from the Bell-Waldron restaurant, and that I could travel to Q.P.R. for the princely sum of £5-70. Tucked away in the corner of page 11 is a small photo of Milan squad player, later to become England Manager, Fabio Capello who looked a dead ringer for Sylvester Stallone.

The Milan side contained the veteran goalkeeper Albertosi, the soon to be great Franco Baresi and the magician Gianni Rivera. But on this night of all nights they had no answer to City's waves of attacks. Asa Hartford took the game by the scruff of the neck pinging the ball out to Mick Channon and particularly Peter Barnes on the wings. Barnes was on fire. They tried to kick him but they could not catch him. Paul Power was living up to his name with surging runs into the heart of the Milan defence. The game was over by half time. Attacking the Platt Lane End City scored three goals without reply with headers from Tommy Booth and Brian Kidd and a shot from Asa Hartford from just inside the penalty area. The atmosphere inside Maine Road that night was as good as I can remember. The crowd was given as 38000 the next day. That could not have been correct. Certainly from my vantage point I could not see any empty seats and you could not move on the Kippax. The Match bus and the 17 back to Middleton passed in a blur and I arrived home exhausted but in a state of absolute euphoria. "Come on you Blue-es"!

The euphoria did not last for long. City's winless run in the League continued throughout a December in which top striker Brian Kidd was absent injured. Ron Futcher tried his best to deliver the goods and there was even a debut for Polish veteran Kasiu Deyna but to no avail. City simply did not look like a team. It was clear that a few injuries revealed the squad to be threadbare. Tueart, Royle and Doyle had all left the club and Colin Bell was struggling with his serious injury. Other players had lost form and the new signings had not really come off. They were not as good as the players that they were brought in to replace. Yet on our day as against Milan the City side showed that it had what it takes to succeed. There was still a strong nucleus of Corrigan, Donachie, Watson, Booth, Owen, Hartford, Power, Channon and Kidd. It only needed three or four experienced signings to keep the club at the top for years. Yet instead of doing this Chairman Peter Swales panicked. Early in the New Year while photographer Kevin Cummins was lining up the band Joy Division for a photograph on the bridge over a snowbound Princess Parkway just a few streets away Malcolm Allison was breezing back into Maine Road.

THREE.

A WINTER OF DISCONTENT.

It was not just on the football field that things looked bleak. Manchester itself was grinding to a halt. The winter of 1978-79 was later to be named the "Winter of Discontent". And for good reason. Strikes were called throughout the land which brought the country to its knees with the army placed on standby. Huge piles of rubbish were building up in the centre of Manchester as the dustbin men went on strike. As thick snow began to fall I had to slalom around mountains of black plastic bin bags on my way to work. Things were even worse in nearby Tameside where even the gravediggers downed their tools! Manchester was greyer than I can ever remember. As the days became shorter it seemed as if it never got really light at all before the night closed in. After work I would stumble up Old Bank Street and descend the stairs into the newly opened "Corbieres" which was owned by Mike Doyle. There were black and white photographs of actors along the bar as "Corbieres" was initially intended as a high class wine bar for the theatre crowd at the nearby Royal Exchange. But this did not last long and in no time at all it began to be frequented by a largely male early twenties crowd attracted by its fantastic juke box. As midnight approached with the sounds of The Clash or maybe Jimi Hendrix ringing in my ears I emerged into the cold night air to make my way to "Rafters", "Pips", or "Cellar V" which all remained open until two o'clock in the morning. I could not afford taxis so at closing time I would crawl up Market Street for the pleasures of the all night bus from Piccadilly back to Middleton. I soon mastered the knack of not making eye contact with anybody on the journey.

At home these were difficult times for mum in particular as all three of her sons began to branch out into the night life of Manchester. I was now twenty years old, brother Pete was nineteen and Paul was just fifteen. Our parents did not stand in our way but warned us all to be careful when out late at night in town. Mum told us years later that she did not fall asleep until all three of us were safely tucked up in bed. Usually we were all in by the early hours a little worse for wear but nothing more. There was one night that did not follow the usual pattern. I made my way into town with two old friends from school, Gary and Steve. After a few pints we found ourselves in the "Swinging Sporran" which was situated on Sackville Street near the Polytechnic round the back of Oxford Road. The music reflected the mixed clientele and had a bit of everything, but as usual by a quarter to two we had not met the girls of our dreams so we slowly made our way outside to the sound of The Commodores who were telling us that it was "Easy like Sunday Morning". What happened next was certainly not easy, even though it was indeed Sunday morning. We stood on the pavement amongst a throng of about fifty clubbers who were all chatting away in a bid to delay the inevitable homecoming. Out of the corner of my eye I caught sight of a group of what appeared to be Teddy boys who seemed to be heading our way. I did not know that Teddy boys still existed some twenty years after their heyday, and reasoned that they must be in fancy dress. However they walked straight at us and sensing the danger I urged the lads not to say anything. They barged right into the three of us knocking us into the road. Instinctively Gary said a couple of words to them, the second of which was "off". They immediately turned on us. I raised my left arm to parry what transpired later to be a chain or some kind of knuckleduster. The lads were not so lucky. The Teds landed blows and seconds later disappeared into the night. Blood was pouring from Gary's face and would not stop. He thought he had a bloody nose or maybe lost a tooth or two but it turned out that he had been stabbed! Steve was wearing a white shirt and white jeans and as he turned his back I could see that his trousers were drenched in blood. He too had received a knife wound in his lower back. All this was over in ten seconds and people around just watched open mouthed. Panic set in as an ambulance duly arrived and the next few hours passed in a blur at Bootle Street police station and Manchester Royal. Two things stand out in my memory. At one point a police officer walked past me in a corridor with the clothes of Steve and Gary in plastic bags. I immediately thought the worst. Then, half an hour or so later, a nurse emerged from behind a bedside curtain, grabbed hold of my arm and dragged me to the bedside of some poor woman who was having her stomach pumped.

"Who the bloody hell is he?" she cried at my confused figure as I simultaneously made a swift exit.

"I am sorry, love" mumbled the nurse. "I thought you were her husband."

The lads were kept in for a couple of days but I am pleased to say that they made a full recovery. I was very shaken by the events of the night and for at least the next couple of months I crossed the road if I saw any group of more than two or three lads walking down the road.

A few weeks later the three of us had to go back down to Bootle Street police station to attend an identity parade. The Teddy boys had been arrested later that same evening as they brutally attacked a couple of middle aged diners on their way out of a restaurant on Deansgate. I had seen lots of identity parades on TV on programmes like "Columbo" and "Kojak" but this was completely different. First of all we had to share a waiting room with the families of several criminals who let us know in no uncertain terms what they would do to us if we "identified" their beloved sons or husbands. Then there was the parade itself. It was not a case of looking at people behind glass. We had to walk along the line inches away from the men! As we did some of the "gentlemen" were shaking uncontrollably and crying with fear in case we put the finger on them. The most bizarre thing of all was that they were all clad in orange, red and blue Teddy boy suits and crepe shoes. They hysterically reminded me of mum's favourite band Showaddywaddy. I expected them to burst into song. "Let's go for a little walk………." I was not able to identify anybody. It had happened in a blur weeks ago.

Snow and ice lay on the ground throughout January as City gained a point at Leeds and lost narrowly at home to Chelsea. At least the F.A. Cup offered some respite as the Blues limped past lowly Rotherham after a replay setting up a Fourth Round tie away at Gay Meadow, the home of Shrewsbury Town. Macker and I duly bought tickets and were pleased to be offered a lift to the match by a friend of his from Manchester University.

"This is them, now" announced Macker as a 1960s green Volkswagen mounted the kerb only inches from our frostbitten toes as we waited anxiously at the end of Kingsway.

"Jump in lads" shouted the driver who must have been in his late forties and a dead ringer for a young David Jason.

"This is Bob from Uni, and this is Don his mate from Ramsbottom", said Macker helpfully.

"Hi fellas", I replied cheerfully. As we left behind the metropolis of Stockport and hit the A49 towards Whitchurch I soon realised that the conversation in the car was as good as any comedy sitcom on television at the time. Bob the driver had his nose to the windscreen and cheerfully told us as the snow began to fall that he could not see a "bloody" thing. He did not pause for breath as his machine gun delivery was punctuated by every swear word under the sun. This was hilarious in itself but even more remarkable when I took into account the fact that he was an ex-vicar studying for a Theology degree.

His mate Don, at least twenty years his senior, played the straight man perfectly and grunted and nodded in agreement at everything that Bob said. They had clearly rehearsed this act. It was brilliant.

"Tell 'em Don how your wife gave you an ultimatum. It was either her or Man City. And you told her that you did love her but you had a season ticket for Maine Road!"

"That's right" mumbled Don. "I have been on my own for a while, now." Macker and I were holding our stomachs. Our hearts were also in our mouths as the Volkswagen went slipping and sliding along the country lanes on the long and winding road to Shrewsbury.

Somehow we made it and parked up near the ground. It was a bitter cold afternoon but at least the wintry sun was breaking through. We saw the man with the rowing boat making his way over the bridge. It was his job to fish the ball out of the river. (I reckoned that he would have needed an ice pick today.) The stands seemed to be supplied by Subbuteo. As we walked along behind the main stand I noticed the Match Of The Day cameras were here. They must have been here for the traditional Cup shock. The Shrewsbury faithful were clad in Harris Tweed and Barbour and carrying hip flasks. They looked as if they would be more at home at Twickenham. They cast anxious glances as the Blue and White Army clad mainly in Donkey jackets and carrying cans of lager filed past chanting "If you hate Man United clap your hands!"

As we entered the Away terrace behind the goal it was disappointing to see that the perimeter fence was almost as high as the stand itself. This meant that you had to watch the game through an iron grill. A sad sign of the times. The pitch that day did resemble a meadow of sorts. But there was nothing gay about it. It was rock hard, covered in some places by snow and others by straw! The City side was at full strength with a forward line of Channon, Deyna, Kidd, Hartford and Barnes. As we lined up in our change kit of white shirts with a red and black sash and black shorts a terrible feeling of dread came over me. Straight from the kick off the ball was hit long over our back four and it was clear that it was almost impossible to turn on this surface. Futcher, never that quick even on a good day, scrambled the ball away for a throw in. The Shrewsbury players and crowd took great heart from this first attack and it was not long before they were peppering our goal area. Standing behind Big Joe in the goal it was clear that the height of the sun at the other end was also causing problems. Our slick passing moves were totally inappropriate and we could not find our men. What was worse was that it seemed to me that some of our so-called stars did not seem up for the game in such Arctic conditions. Deyna seemed to be going through the motions and was withdrawn at half time. Yet he had over a hundred caps for Poland! He must have played in these conditions all his life. Eventually the inevitable happened. Shrewsbury scored and the place erupted. You just knew that City were not going to get back in the game. The players seemed to accept the inevitable and looked to blame the pitch for the eventual defeat. Shortly before the end Shrewsbury got another and we were out of the Cup. Typical City. A team of internationals humbled by lowly Shrewsbury. On our return journey Bob did not exactly use such words to convey his disappointment. Don must have wished that he had chosen the missus. I was just glad to get back home in one piece, and my mum and dad could not understand why I wanted to watch it again on Match Of The Day. There are some things that words cannot explain.

Tony Book retained the title of Manager but I can only guess as to how much influence he had on bringing Malcolm Allison back to Maine Road. Chairman Peter Swales was blind in his pursuit of not only putting City on a par with great rivals United but also overtaking them and becoming the biggest club in both domestic and world football. But having brought Malcolm back to the club Swales and Book must shoulder the responsibility for what happened next. At first Malcolm tried to revitalise the training regime and indeed the few players who remained from his first successful stint at the club were initially pleased to see him back after six years away. But after the Shrewsbury defeat and an embarrassing three goal reverse to United in the League things began to slowly slip away. It was the manner of the defeat to the Reds that hurt the most. On another rock hard surface at Maine Road City surrendered feebly and the game was over as a contest after a mere thirty five minutes with two blockbusters from Steve Coppell. The rest of the match was like a testimonial and when Andy Ritchie scored a third on sixty eight minutes I uncharacteristically left the ground early, deeply saddened by what I had seen. Unsurprisingly I had not been able to persuade any of the lads to attend this match after the Cup defeat at Shrewsbury.

There were still occasional highlights, or false dawns I guess. After a blank Saturday I set off alone for my first ever visit to Highfield Road, the home of Coventry City. I decided to catch an early train from Piccadilly avoiding the Football Specials and by doing so any potential trouble. I had to change at Birmingham New Street and even though it was only about eleven o'clock it resembled a war zone. There seemed to be hundreds of police with dogs on the concourse and on the various platforms separating rival gangs of thugs on their way to matches throughout the Midlands that day. I sported no colours and did not ally myself to any large group of lads. If things ever got hairy I buried my head in the New Musical Express, Sounds or Melody Maker and tried to give the impression of being a music geek rather than a hired assassin. I arrived in Coventry about midday and found what I used to call an "old man's pub" in the city centre near the bombed out Cathedral. This was a pub that served good beer and did not have a jukebox or a pool table. Thus nobody under forty ever came in. Apart from me of course! A pie and a pint or two later I found myself outside the away end as the gates were about to open. It was absolutely freezing. I glanced to my left to see the Mercer Arms named of course after our Joe. I nodded to several Blues milling around whom I recognised from my travels around the country. I entered the ground, bought a programme and must have read it from cover to cover at least three times before a slightly subdued travelling support cheered their heroes onto the pitch. Colin Viljoen returned to the team in place of Bell and it was great to see Tommy Booth back in defence. Big Mal had clearly been tinkering with the formation. I had never seen anything like it as City packed the midfield and played with two wingers, Channon and Barnes, but with nobody up front! Coventry's central defenders had nobody to mark and for the whole of the first half they simply looked at each other. Incredibly City won the game by three goals to nil with two from Mick Channon and one from a deep lying Brian Kidd. Although I did not know this at the time this turned out to be Brian's last goal for the Blues. It was also only our seventh victory from twenty six league games. Nevertheless I danced my way through Birmingham New Street on my way home that night!

The first signs that Malcolm Allison had returned to the club with a distinct agenda became clear to all true Blues when the side was announced for the vitally important UEFA Cup quarter final against Borussia Monchengladbach. He selected untried youngsters Nicky Reid and Tony Henry while leaving the experienced Brian Kidd, Colin Bell and Kasiu Deyna on the bench. The first leg at Maine Road was a tight affair so typical of many European ties with City holding the lead for long periods before having to settle for a draw, but the second leg was totally one-sided with Borussia coming out on top by three goals to one.

Just over a week later Brian Kidd was sold to Everton. I was devastated and somewhat bewildered to see him go. Despite his obvious Old Trafford connections

Kiddo was universally welcomed by all City fans and gave everything he had to the City cause. His goalscoring record was second to none. In a high flying entertaining side Brian scored 57 goals from 127 games. What is more he was a good North Manchester lad and always had time for the fans unlike so many others in top class football. The City side began to take on an unfamiliar look as new signing Barry Silkman, Nicky Reid, Tony Henry, and Kasiu Deyna all became regulars. Colin Bell was deployed as sweeper. Deyna hit the goal trail by banging in five as City won five of their last six home matches to preserve their First Division status.

FOUR.

LONDON CALLING.

Early that summer I was summoned to the Manager's office at work. He told me that with immediate effect I was being transferred to the Moston branch in the suburbs. I was hugely disappointed as I loved working in the city centre. It was great nipping into pubs like the Nags Head off Deansgate with its coffin for a table and Tommy Ducks near The Midland Hotel with its knickers on the wall. I loved thumbing through the racks in the record shops on Market Street at lunchtime. Occasionally we would go to Manchester Press Club to play snooker. I was amazed that members got in by using "swipe card technology". This must have been years ahead of its time in the late seventies. The club was packed and through the dim haze of smoke above the immaculate green baize many an important financial deal was brokered. I soon realised that the managers completed most of their work in the office in the morning before disappearing for long lunches. If they did return in late afternoon it was usual that they placed a "Do not disturb" sign on their office doors.

I was not the only man being transferred that summer. To the amazement and general bewilderment of all City fans Malcolm Allison got rid of the best two prospects to have come out of the City junior sides in years. Peter Barnes and Gary Owen were sensationally sold to West Bromwich Albion. It was reported that Owen was in tears as he left the club. God only knows what was going on in the corridors of Maine Road. Worse was to come. Incredibly Asa Hartford and the majestic Dave Watson were allowed to leave followed closely by Mick Channon and Kenny Clements. Why was nobody big enough behind the scenes to stand up and at least voice their disapproval at the events which were unfolding that summer? I cannot believe, as some have since suggested, that Malcolm could not handle established pros like Kidd, Hartford, Watson and Channon. If he had simply decided to get rid of the old order this did not explain his decision to get rid of Owen and Barnes from the club. In order to replace these stars City paid out big money for "untried" youngsters such as Mackenzie and Robinson, and promoted sixteen year old Tommy Caton into the first team. Dragoslav Stepanovic who allegedly did not speak English was appointed Captain. Some fans argued that Mal was trying to replicate what he and Joe Mercer did in 1965 by building a team from nothing. But back then Mal and Joe did not dismantle a good City side full of internationals. It says so much for City's fantastic support that there was a crowd of 40000 for the opening fixture against Crystal Palace. Needless to say it was a terrible game and both sides were lucky to get nil! Steve Daley was recruited from Wolves for a club record of £1,450,000 and after six games City were bottom of the league.

Three home wins had catapulted the Blues to sixteenth by the time United arrived at Maine Road on November the 10th. The Reds were a point clear of Nottingham Forest at the top of the League and contained in their ranks South African goalkeeper Gary Bailey, defenders Kevin Moran and Martin Buchan, and attackers Sammy McIlroy, Ray Wilkins, Steve Coppell and Lou Macari. I was by now attending not only away games but also home games alone. I do not know if Macker and Phil were losing interest but it was clear that they were finding other things to do on their Saturday afternoons. I decided to purchase a seat in the Main Stand even though I had a season ticket on the Kippax. I managed to get a seat about a dozen rows from the front just to the left of the player's tunnel as I looked at the pitch. This was directly opposite where I stood week after week on the Kippax terraces, and I watched with interest as the huge stand opposite filled up as kick off approached. As I looked around me it was clear that the fans were extremely keyed up and as fervent as those on the terraces. But there was certainly something missing. It was just not the same in the seats. Maybe it was because there was more room. It was not as physical. In the build-up to kick off I glanced through the programme and two things took my eye. First of all there was a new team picture which was really unusual. They normally appear in August, but I guess there were so many comings and goings that they did not actually get around to doing one! Even club stalwarts Booth, Donachie and Power had the look of condemned men in the line-up. The second thing that took my eye was a letter from a fan who asked why Kenny Clements had been sold to Oldham. The reply from Malcolm Allison gave a rare insight on his thoughts at the time concerning the hiring and firing of players. Malcolm stated that he felt that all the players should be "capable of reaching international standard" and that he felt that Kenny was not and that this is why he let him go. This reasoning is all well and good but was not backed up by the signings of Daley, Lee, and Silkman among others and the promotion of Henry and Reid, none of whom came anywhere near international standard. Significantly Malcolm added that Tony Book did not agree with him.

The teams took to the field and straight from the kick off the cornerstones of the City side such as Corrigan, Booth, Donachie and Power played with calm assurance, and youngsters Ranson, Bennett, Caton and Robinson chased down every ball with great enthusiasm. The spirits of the City fans who had feared the worst were steadily rising as the game wore on. The teams were level at half time and City were giving a good account of themselves. The rain started to fall and the pitch began to cut up as the Blues attacked the North Stand. On the hour mark Deyna weaved his way through the United defence and the ball ran loose. It seemed to take an age as it rolled across the penalty area. Tony Henry swung his left leg and City were one up! I leapt to my feet as the crowd went wild. I glanced around to see that some fans dotted around the stand had not moved. They must have been Reds. I regained my composure and looked across at the swaying mass on the Kippax. How I wished that I was there. Minutes later Robinson scored another, Helen rang her bell and we were home and dry. A famous victory! We celebrated long into the night.

The punks had by now largely disappeared from the streets of Manchester. Those in the know would claim that punk rock had started with the two Sex Pistols gigs in June 1976 at the Lesser Free Trade Hall and had blown away with the closure of the Electric Circus just eighteen months later. Standard bearers like The Clash, The Stranglers and The Jam moved into the mainstream and Johnny Rotten had become John Lydon and formed The Public Image. Winds of change were blowing from other directions. Two Tone Records from the Midlands brought a revival of ska and reggae with the fantastic Specials, The Selector and of course Madness. There was also a huge Mod revival with the release of The Who film "Quadrophenia". The Who themselves had launched a nationwide tour no doubt to capitalise on the success of the film. There were no gigs in Manchester but on a dark November Friday night I found myself on the train from Piccadilly with fellow Blue Dave Lamb en route for New Bingley Hall in Stafford. We made the concert with minutes to spare and managed to push our way to within ten yards of the stage as Pete Townshend thrashed out the opening chords. I looked around. The crowd was ninety nine per cent male, clad mainly in parkas despite the heat and swaying like the Kippax on a European match night. The atmosphere was tremendous and it was just so loud! John Entwhistle pounded out the bass lines, new drummer Kenney Jones was doing his level best to replace recently deceased legend Keith Moon, while Roger Daltrey flailed his microphone above his head. We made the last train with minutes to spare. As I tumbled in through the front door at such an unearthly hour, exhausted, my ears ringing, and a little worse for wear, mum whispered "Good night, son. I hope you enjoyed it."

City were in freefall. After two good wins before Christmas against Derby and Everton the Blues went seventeen games without a win in the League and were dumped out of the F.A. Cup by lowly Halifax. I am pleased to state that I missed this game. Let's just say that after Shrewsbury the year before I had a gut feeling. By March even the loyal left back Willie Donachie decided it was time to go as he left for the United States bitterly lamenting the state of his beloved club. But at last we had something to cheer about when Dennis Tueart made the trip in the opposite direction to re-sign for the club. The team though was much weaker than when he left and I felt that upon his return he had lost a yard or so of his electric pace. Nevertheless it was great to see him again and he was joined by million pound signing Kevin Reeves. Reeves had a great reputation but seemed a little timid to me, rather like most Norwich City players. I cannot believe that he cost a million pounds! But he chipped in with a couple of goals and Tueart banged in four as City managed to win three of the last four games and managed to stay in the First Division.

Moston Lane was way past its heyday in 1980 but still recognisable as a village community. It reminded me of Paul McCartney's Penny Lane even though I never saw any pretty nurses selling poppies from a tray. Nevertheless you could set your watch by Mrs. Fox from the cake shop as she casually walked up the lane with the day's takings in her shopping bag while stopping to say hello to all and sundry. I did not need to lift my head up to know when the man from the fish shop came into the bank just before lunch. Counting his one pound notes was painstaking, stuck together as they usually were with vinegar. Norbert Kelly would pop in on his way home from morning mass at Saint Dunstan's, Fred Eyre Senior would smile as he discussed the latest events down at City, as did Mr. Goggins the local headteacher as he arrived late afternoon with the children's dinner money. There were reminders that not everybody in the community shared this romantic vision of life on the lane. The pens in the bank were ripped from their chains on the counter and the Sooty Bear charity boxes disappeared on a daily basis. "Ram raids" at the local T.V. shop brought this new phrase into my vocabulary. Lunchtimes were spent playing pool and eating sausage butties in the Museum public house next door.

As a rule I did not attend pre-season friendly or testimonial matches. But something possessed me to go along to Maine Road to watch the game against Legia Warsaw on August the 12th a few days before the season opened. I guess the game must have been part of the deal which brought Polish Captain Kaziu Deyna to City. Macker, Phil and I stood amongst a sparse crowd on the Kippax as a respectful round of applause announced the arrival of the teams. The Poles seemed content to pass the ball around without really going anywhere. We could not get the ball off them. As soon as they realised what a poor side we were they started to advance upon our penalty area. The Poles proceeded to dance through our static defence as they absolutely hammered us by five goals to one. On the bus back into town the lads said that it was a fluke and that it did not really matter. But deep down I realised that we were a really weak side and that there may be trouble ahead. I did not have to wait too long for my suspicions to be confirmed when in the opening home game lowly Sunderland ran rings around us to win by four goals to nil. I cannot ever remember such an abject performance in the first home game of a season. This was to be the last game of Stepanovic's brief career as City played four centre halves in the back four. Up front Kevin Reeves toiled manfully alongside the incredibly lightweight Paul Sugrue who had been signed from Nuneaton Borough! We had got rid of England International strikers Royle, Tueart and Kidd and were bringing in non- league players as replacements! Thankfully, Sugrue was to make only six appearances in the sky blue shirt. Our agony was not to last much longer when after ten winless games Malcolm Allison was sacked.

New manager John Bond came from the same West Ham academy as Big Mal and had been working miracles down at Norwich City. But it would be true to say that the fans did not really know what to expect. After all, we had had to put up with so much in these last two seasons. Our team was a pale shadow of the side which finished runners up to Liverpool by one point just three short years ago. Bond, though, was a similar charismatic figure to Mal and he made an immediate impact. Like every fan who watches a team regularly it did not take him long to see what the team needed. There was no left back, the midfield lacked bite, and for a Manchester City team there was very little flair on show. Within a fortnight tough tackling full back Bobby McDonald was signed from Coventry, warhorse Gerry Gow from Bristol City and veteran wingman Tommy Hutchison brought his bag of tricks to Maine Road. Million pound misfit Steve Daley did not play again and the whole atmosphere around the club changed. The youngsters like Ranson, Reid, Caton, Mackenzie and Bennett suddenly threw off their shackles and lead boots and began to play with flair and freedom. Bond had supplied the experience that had been missing but crucially he provided that elusive quality of confidence. After initial defeat in his first game at home to Birmingham courtesy of a late penalty the Blues did not look back.

Even two consecutive wins did not initially lift the Blues from 21st place in the table but the first real sign that the times were changing came in the League Cup Tie at home to Notts County on a foul night at the end of October. All the new signings were ineligible for the cup tie but significantly Steve Daley was not selected. Bond preferred the untried youngster Gary Buckley to the million pound misfit. City played with a rediscovered style and grace with Dennis Tueart banging in four goals as the Blues romped home by five goals to one.

Tommy Booth returned for the home game with Southampton a fortnight later. Yet in the first half the rediscovered fluency was somehow missing. The game matched the November weather as City struggled to penetrate the Saints back four. The minutes ticked by and the crowd grew nervous. Had the revival been a mere flash in the pan? There was always the danger of a breakaway and a narrow home defeat. Suddenly Tommy Hutchison picked up the ball on the half way line, jinked past two defenders and set off towards the Platt Lane End with the ball seemingly attached to his twinkling toes. The whole stadium lifted as one as the ball reached Gerry Gow who drilled the ball home. The team was galvanised and the ball was passed out to Hutchison on the right wing at every opportunity. He tore Southampton apart in a breathless display of artistry. Further goals from Kevin Reeves and Dave Bennett gave City a solid victory which had seemed highly unlikely for at least the first hour of the game. The following week Coventry City turned up in what is possibly the worst football kit that I have ever seen. Chocolate brown shirts, shorts and socks. If ever the colour of a team's kit mirrored their performance on the field then this was the one! Yet their side contained the formidable forward pairing of Mark Hately and Gary Thompson ably supported by the wing play of Peter Bodak and Steve Hunt. Their back four included a young Gary Gillespie, veteran Mick Coop and behind them the eccentric Les Sealey. In his programme column John Bond revealed his intention to sign his son Kevin from Norwich City (my heart sank immediately) while talking up Kevin Reeves and praising the brilliant wing play of Tommy Hutchison. City hit their stride straight away. The back four was well balanced and solid as a rock. Gow anchored the midfield which allowed Steve Mackenzie to flourish while Paul Power and Tommy Hutchison tore them apart down the flanks. City could have scored five or six but had to again settle for three with goals from Power, Bennett and Reeves. The league table revealed that City were now in 18th place and that their average home attendance of 32000 was bettered only by Liverpool, Arsenal and Man United. In fact thirteen clubs in the top flight could only average between 15000 and 22000 for their home games. This was a clear reflection of not only the dour football on offer but also the problem of crowd hooliganism which continued to blight the game and keep women and children away from the terraces.

These first games under John Bond carried an extra edge for me in that I travelled to them from my new home in London! Earlier in the summer I had answered an advertisement for a job at Heathrow Airport and to my complete astonishment was successful at interview. I could not have timed it any worse as I left behind not only my close family and group of friends but also a resurgent Manchester City! I drove away from Middleton with a heavy heart on the last day of October 1980 heading for The Heathrow Ambassador Hotel on the Bath Road some five hours away. The lump in my throat soon became a brick in my stomach as I passed the familiar service stations which I had done so many times on Yelloway and Finglands coaches on the way to watch City away matches. Sandbach, Keele, Hilton Park and others passed in a blur as I carefully negotiated my way south in my yellow Datsun which I had bought off dad a couple of weeks before. Needless to say I got lost soon after leaving the motorway at Watford but eventually I arrived at my destination, dropped my case and headed for the bar. I tried to make conversation with one guy who told me he was from Mars. He meant the chocolate factory down the road in Slough but I felt as if I had landed on another planet.

I had to work four day twelve hour shifts with four days off in between. I left for work in the dark and returned in the dead of night. Things were desperate. The job was deadly boring and my colleagues even more so. After a couple of weeks I moved into a room in the Peggy Bedford pub which was so near to the runway that I could open my window and shake hands with the pilot as he came in to land. The room cost me five pounds a week so it was certainly not the Ritz. When I was on the early shift I got back around six in the evening so decided to go down to the bar. The same fellows came in each night separately, each sitting on a stool at the bar alongside me, but not a word was exchanged all night between any of them as they all drank in silence before leaving at last orders. This went on night after night. The only time I managed to get one guy to open up he told me that he was a Chelsea supporter with a passionate hatred for all things Mancunian except for the night that Chelsea beat Leeds at Old Trafford in the F.A. Cup final replay. It did not take me long to realise that I had dropped an absolute clanger coming down here. At the end of my four day shift instead of exploring my new surroundings I hit the road back up North.

"John Lennon has been shot dead in New York", said dad to my brothers downstairs as they prepared to go off to school and university. I was still half asleep in bed and in that strange state between sleep and waking could not believe what I was hearing. The look on my brothers' faces around the breakfast table confirmed my worst fears. We had grown up with the Beatles although we were just a bit too young to be gripped by Beatlemania. My first memories of them was of one of our friend's mums singing what turned out to be "Can't Buy Me Love" as she put the washing out. I have vague recollections of watching The Beatles perform their later singles such as "Lady Madonna", "Hey Jude" and "Let It Be" on "Top of The Pops". The television news revealed that John had been shot by a deranged fan Mark Chapman. There were interviews with grief stricken Gerry Marsden and Cilla Black on Granada Reports, and the radio began to play back to back Beatles records without any commentary in between. It was as if a Head of State or member of The Royal Family had died. A simple sentence from dad had turned my world on its head. I could not face the long drive down to Heathrow so instead caught the afternoon train from Manchester Piccadilly. Up early the next morning I bought every newspaper that I could lay my hands on and immersed myself somewhat morbidly in all things Lennon. I caught a glimpse of Ringo Starr making his way through the Terminal on his way to New York, him being the only Beatle to do so. Time seemed to stand still on the Sunday as there were massive outpourings of grief in both Liverpool and New York in special ceremonies for John.

I boarded the train at London Euston straight after my shift and found myself in the buffet bar. Glancing to my left I recognised former Piccadilly Radio D.J. Andy Peebles who used to do the requests and announcements over the tannoy system at Maine Road. I half-heartedly gave him a weak smile of recognition as one Blue to another. How I wish now that I had engaged him in conversation as it later emerged that he was the last person to interview John Lennon the previous weekend only days before his murder. The single released by John Lennon to mark the appearance of "Double Fantasy" was a celebration entitled "(Just like) Starting Over". I felt that this was just what I had to do. I swallowed my pride and gave my notice in at the Airport. I needed to be back among my loved ones in Manchester.

The Smith's Arms in 2007.

FIVE.

THE SMITHS ARMS.

There was an unusual feeling of optimism in the air at the beginning of 1981. After years of standing against night club walls invisible to the female population of Manchester I was actually recognised by one of them and before I knew it I had a girlfriend! We would meet on a Friday night like thousands of others outside Woolworths before sitting "as a couple" in one of the numerous bars off Piccadilly before venturing down to "Pips" on Fennel Street which I had frequented some years earlier. Jon Richmond from school no longer manned the decks but the Bowie and Roxy room was still as cool as I remembered. As we wandered through the streets hand in hand I would look in the windows of every parked car and shop window just to make sure that it was really me!

Things were also looking up at Maine Road. Three consecutive victories left the Blues in thirteenth place in the League, this being their highest position so far. The third round of the F.A. Cup paired City with Malcolm Allison's Crystal Palace. The City side was unrecognisable to the one that he had left behind three short months ago. Incredibly the main difference was one of confidence which was certainly not something that Mal himself was short of. Indeed in a remarkable display of self-confidence just before kick-off Mal ran across the pitch with his arms outstretched to meet the acclamation of the hordes on the Kippax. And we in turn gave him a rousing reception, which was quite strange really considering what he had recently put us all through. Palace though performed like City of old and the Blues cruised to a 4-0 victory with goals from Kevin Reeves (2), Paul Power and new signing Phil Boyer. The draw for the next round paired City with John Bond's old side Norwich City but before then we had the mouth- watering prospect of a League Cup Semi Final first leg against the mighty Liverpool to look forward to.

The first sign that the night would not be too straight forward was when we saw the size of the queues for the Match buses on Aytoun Street. The rain began to fall as we inched forward. I looked across at the outline of the former Grand Hotel and thought momentarily of all the amorous assignations that would have taken place there behind the now soot blackened windows. I checked my watch. It was ten past six. We had plenty of time yet. Eventually we boarded the bus and arrived at Maine Road with at least forty minutes to go. The crowds were heavy as we ran along the back of the North Stand before turning the corner into the Kippax Car Park. My heart immediately sank. There were few cars or coaches. Just people as far as the eye could see. I had never seen queues like this at Maine Road in my life. It was cold, dark, wet and indeed there was a feeling of high tension in the air as kick off approached. We did not seem to be getting any nearer to the turnstiles. The only other time I had experienced something like this was at Anfield in 1977 and on that day I was locked out of the ground. It was clear that City had miscalculated the size of the crowd. Sure, the seats were all ticket, but why not the Kippax? After all, this was a semi- final against the mighty Liverpool. Fans were becoming really angry and police horses were brought in to control the vast crowds. The eerie glow from the floodlights and the roars of the people who had managed to get in the ground only heightened the tension. The "oohs" and the "aahs" marked the progress of the Blues on the pitch as the queue inched forward. All of a sudden there was a huge roar! We were one up! Macker and I did not find out until later that Kevin Reeves had the ball in the net but it was disallowed. There were no mobile phones in 1981! Even years later arguments raged that this goal should have stood. Incredibly we did not get in until half time! We managed to stand in the tunnel but could not get onto the actual terracing. I was surprised to read in the Express the next day that the crowd was given as 48045. This was four thousand below capacity! I am sure they just used to make it up. City were without MacDonald, Gow and Hutchison who were ineligible and replaced them with Tony Henry, Dave Bennett and Dennis Tueart. I only saw half the game but as far as I could see the Blues absolutely controlled the game but could not get the ball past Clemence in the Liverpool goal. Shortly before the end the inevitable happened as Liverpool broke away and Ray Kennedy scored the only goal of the game. As I trudged in the front door shortly after eleven mum greeted me cheerily but deep in my heart I knew that it would take a miracle to overcome Liverpool at Anfield by two goals. There were no dreams of Wembley that night.

I had no time to stew over the club's ineptitude over the ticketing arrangements or the gross injustice of the manner of defeat. The big matches were coming thick and fast. A home draw with mighty Notts Forest was followed by a magnificent performance in the second leg at Anfield. Despite the Blues laying siege to the Liverpool goal the Scousers held on for a one all draw and it was they and not us who would be going out to try on their Wembley suits in the next few days. Instead we had a tricky Fifth Round tie away at Peterborough on Valentine's Day. John Bond had no hesitation in recalling his trio of Gow, Hutchison and McDonald. Surprisingly young Tommy Caton, Buckley and Tueart stood down from the side which had performed so heroically at Anfield. The game was a tight affair decided by a goal from Middleton born Tommy Booth recalling his winner in the semi- final over Everton some twelve years earlier.

We began to establish a new match day routine in those early days under John Bond. We said farewell to the Match bus on Aytoun Street as both Phil and I now had cars, and Macker returned the compliment by borrowing his dad's. We would drive down through Collyhurst and call in for a pre-match pint at the Smith's Arms behind the

Daily Express. Unfortunately along with his dad's car Macker was also entrusted with taking along his little brother Peter from time to time, who must have been no older than about eight! When we got to the Smith's Arms, known to one and all as the "Hammer" we were faced with a dilemma. It was unheard of in those days to take children into a pub and as for The Hammer it would have been unthinkable, packed as it was with hard seasoned drinkers. In fact it was rare to come across a woman in there unless she was working behind the bar. Macker opened the glove compartment and joyfully produced an English dictionary.

"Here you are, Peter. You have a read of this while we go in to the pub!"

We enjoyed our drinks as we discussed the afternoon's prospects and Peter learnt a few new words every fortnight. The ideal solution!

Young Peter had to be left at home for the derby as United were beaten one nil with a goal from Steve Mackenzie at the Platt Lane End after a strong run down the left and cross by Paul Power. The fact that we did not go completely over the top at this result illustrated our growing confidence in the Blues. We did not know that this would be the last victory over the Reds for some eight years. We also thought that our major chance of glory that season was yet to come with only Everton standing between ourselves and an F.A. Cup semi final. At Goodison Park the two sides shared the spoils in a two all draw with Paul Power equalising for the Blues with only five or six minutes left on the clock. In a typical cup tie the Sunday Mirror reported that "City and Everton had been perfectly matched with bruise for bruise, kick for kick, and charge for charge".

The replay was fixed for Wednesday the 11th March and we decided to leave the cars at home and go back on the bus for this one. We had no intention of being caught out as we were some weeks earlier for the Liverpool game so we arranged to meet on Aytoun Street for the Match bus at five o'clock. The script could already have been written as steady rain started to fall as the night closed in on Piccadilly Gardens. Office workers were huddled under their umbrellas idly chattering as they waited for their buses home. The Evening News seller on the corner confirmed that Tommy Hutchison was fit to face the scousers. As we turned the corner a quick glance revealed that the early start had done the trick. The queues for the buses were pretty small and in no time at all we were marching across the forecourt by the Ticket Office.

"Did you notice there were quite a few scousers on the bus?" asked Macker innocently. It was packed with them in truth but I did not say anything. Everton had a really strong fan base with a great away following and it would be true to say that in the late 1970s tensions usually ran high between both sets of fans. As kick off approached the atmosphere on the Kippax was electric. There was something special about night matches, with the air of menace usually present in the early Eighties really heightening the tension. There was a huge sense of anticipation for this one. City were at full strength apart from the suspended Tommy Booth. In front of Joe Corrigan was a back four of Ray Ranson, Nicky Reid, Tommy Caton and Bobby McDonald. In midfield stopper Gerry Gow was flanked by Steve Mackenzie and wingers Tommy Hutchison and Paul Power. Up front Dennis Tueart played off Kevin Reeves. Everton's experienced line up contained a number of past and future Blues in John Gidman, Steve McMahon, Imre Varadi and Asa Hartford. The ground was packed to capacity with an official attendance of 52,532. The Blues did not let us down. They produced a vintage display of skill combined with controlled aggression which totally blew away their opponents. Everton in their change yellow strip could not handle the wizardry of Tommy Hutchison on the right wing, the strength of Gow through the middle and the strong running of Tueart and Reeves in attack. Yet it was the unsung hero at full back Bobby McDonald who scored two of the three goals on the night. The other was converted by skipper Paul

Power who was in the form of his life. As the third goal went in there was a huge surge in the Kippax as absolute strangers embraced with unfettered joy as only a football crowd could. We soon regained our place on the terrace but we could not contain our joy as we marched through the rain sodden back streets of Moss Side and onto our buses into town. "Wem-berlee, Wem-berlee, We're the famous Man City and we're going to Wem-ber-lee".

Three days later we were back at Maine Road to witness the debut of City's young black goalkeeper Alex Williams against West Bromwich Albion. Racism was rife in football and the National Front was in regular attendance outside many First Division grounds but not Maine Road as far as I was aware. Elsewhere black players were jeered mercilessly and often booed whenever they touched the ball. There seemed to be less of this at City perhaps due to the fact that the Blues played in Moss Side or maybe because City had a reputation for giving black youngsters a chance. Indeed, along with Williams, Dave Bennett and Roger Palmer were members of the first team squad. Nevertheless, the goalkeeper is a vulnerable position on a football field at the best of times so we were very impressed by the courage of young Alex Williams. The crowd got behind him from the kick off and the Blues ran out winners by two goals to one against a team who three years earlier famously contained the brilliant trio of black players Cyrille Regis, Laurie Cunningham and Brendan Batson. This was to be City's last win for four weeks as the F.A. Cup paired them with Bobby Robson's high flying Ipswich Town in the semi final which was due to take place at Villa Park on April 11th.

It was agreed that it was my turn to drive down to Birmingham. I had no confidence in my Mazda car ever reaching the Midlands let alone bringing us back in one piece. I had been "conned" into buying it from a garage in Moston. They said it was the "Car of the Week" but which particular week I am not too sure. Let's just say that they must have seen me coming. My brother Pete revealed years later that the whole family were embarrassed to see it parked outside our house let alone to be actually seen in it! However we set off on that fine spring morning and we only ground to a halt along with everybody else on the motorway about ten miles outside Birmingham. The traffic was gridlocked to such an extent that some Blues from a mini bus actually got out and played football in between the cars! We had plenty of time so it was a huge laugh at first. Half an hour later we had not moved and the tension had started to rise. Young Peter looked up from his dictionary to ask why we were not moving. The reply was less than charitable! Eventually we were up and running through the infamous Spaghetti Junction and we caught a glimpse of the distinctive floodlights to our right. We parked up behind the Witton End, and made our way through the dense crowds to the giant Holte End terraces. As I entered the ground to the right of the goalposts and looked across the pitch at the rapidly filling stadium I felt the same rush of adrenalin as I did on my first visit to Maine Road with dad in 1966. Yes, today was that special. I was surrounded by best mates Phil and Macker, young Peter, and my young brother Paul was in the Witton End behind the other goal. The Blues had half of both ends behind the goals with a large section of seats to our left. The atmosphere in the Holte end that day was absolutely magnificent and I held aloft my Red and Black scarf with great pride. Even though we were the underdogs it never entered my head that we would not win.

The Blues were at full strength with Dave Bennett replacing Dennis Tueart being the only change from the side that faced Everton in the quarter finals. Ipswich were flying high in the First Division. In fact this was probably their greatest ever side. They were captained by Mick Mills, one of the few footballers that my mum recognised, who she referred to as a "young executive". I think she felt that he seemed like a nice boy, a feeling echoed in the programme by England Manager Ron Greenwood. The centre back pairing of Osman and Butcher was formidable, the midfield of Thijssen, Muhren, Wark and Gates had everything, and the strikers Mariner and Brazil were full of goals. With so much talent on the pitch a goal fest was on the cards. Instead what we got was a war of attrition which seemed to be heading for a replay. Until that is, deep in extra time City were awarded a free kick just outside the area right in front of us down at the Holte End. Perhaps Tommy Hutchison would curl it into the corner, or maybe Steve Mackenzie would blast it through the wall like Franny Lee in his pomp. I groaned inwardly as instead Paul Power shaped up to take it. I mean I don't think he had ever taken a free kick before. The ground absolutely erupted after a milli-second of silence as the ball nestled in the corner of the net. Youngsters Tommy Caton and Nicky Reid raced over to the sky blue hordes and would have jumped into the crowd if they could have done. We screamed our heads off! Pat Partridge blew his whistle and City were at Wembley. Strangers embraced, I was kissed on the cheek, and we set off for Manchester in a haze, or was it a Mazda? Somewhere near Walsall there was a huge commotion as the Man United team bus came flying past in the third lane with their curtains closed on a sunny evening hoping to avoid recognition from the thousands of celebratory Blues. While we had reached Wembley they were merely fulfilling a meaningless League fixture somewhere in the Midlands.

My job in London the previous autumn meant that I had not renewed my Kippax season ticket and this was now to cause me unforeseen problems. In the past I would simply have sent in the form from my season ticket book to get a Wembley ticket. As the weeks went by with the season ticket deadline over and my failure to collect enough vouchers from the programmes it seemed that my chances were slim. Dad asked around in the pub for me but everybody with club connections were being bombarded anyway. Then one morning before work he announced that he could get me a ticket. Unfortunately though, he reasoned it would have to be from a ticket tout and for a much inflated price. With only a week to go it was my only chance. So one frosty early evening I made my way round to a very nice bungalow somewhere on the posh Alkrington estate and rang the bell. A matronly lady who looked as if she had been baking cakes all afternoon answered with a cheery smile, asked me to step in, and then in a wholly different kind of tone asked me out of the corner of her mouth if I had the exact money. I handed over thirty five pounds which was ten times the asking price of a terrace ticket and which represented a huge two weeks wages. She counted it out in front of me and disappeared into the dining room where I could just make out a shadowy figure sat at the table. Few words were exchanged as the transaction was completed. She returned, handed me the ticket and ushered me out of the door and onto the streets. Without a backward glance I scurried away into the shadows like a murderer fleeing the scene of the crime. High on adrenalin with a huge feeling of exhilaration I breathlessly made my getaway with the ticket firmly clenched in my left hand until I reached the safety of home. I checked the ticket over and over every night before going to sleep, and was not wholly convinced that it was genuine until I handed it over at the turnstiles on Saturday the ninth of May. There was no hand on my shoulder or "Excuse me, sir?" as I slipped away in the direction of a programme seller some yards from the turnstile.

The programme which set me back 80 pence reminded me that it was the One Hundredth F.A. Cup Final. I took up my place alone at the tunnel end as I did in 1974 and 1976. It seemed strange not to be accompanied by Macker and Phil this time. They too did not have a season ticket, or even the opportunity to take part in any "criminal activity" like myself. In his programme notes John Bond revealed that if he had any sense he would resign from his post as he would not be able to achieve what he had in the last seven months with the Blues. He pointed to the fact that City had preserved their

First Division status, reached the semi-finals of the League Cup and now the Final of the F.A. Cup. He also thanked the senior players Joe Corrigan, Paul Power and Tommy Booth for their help and influence in those first few weeks. But it was clear that his signings of Hutchison, Gow and MacDonald were master strokes. Turning to the team sheets in the centre of the programme I noticed that Ray Ranson's name was not spelt correctly and that Spurs would include the Argentinian pairing of Ricardo Villa and Ossie Ardiles in their ranks. It had been rumoured some months earlier that City had first option to sign them both but did not fancy Ricky Villa. How differently things may have turned out! My only disappointment was that Middleton born Tommy Booth had not made the starting line-up. Like many finals the game itself was unremarkable and thanks to a rare header from Tommy Hutch seemed to be going City's way. Just as they were getting the sky blue ribbon ready to attach to the Cup a needless free kick was given away just outside our box. One of those "typical City" moments! I felt it in my stomach as the wall lined up. Glenn Hoddle curled it around the wall where it hit Tommy Hutchison and ricocheted into the opposite corner of the net past a helpless Joe Corrigan. A draw! Tommy Hutch had transformed our season but he would be forever remembered as the player who scored for both teams in a Wembley final. After watching so many finals on television since childhood it seemed really strange not to see a captain lift the Cup. With no winner both teams made a subdued lap of honour. This strange sensation continued as I left the ground along with the two sets of fans before boarding a tube carriage full of Spurs supporters for the short journey into central London. Due to the extortionate price that I had paid for my ticket I could not afford to attend the replay on the Thursday night. Instead I watched in horror along with millions of others on T.V. as Ricky Villa seemed to run past the whole City team over and over again as in a nightmare before planting the winner firmly past a bemused Joe Corrigan.

The sky was red as Moss Side burned that summer. Petrol bombs rained down on the thin blue line of police officers as looters helped themselves from smashed shop windows all along Market Street in the city centre with damage to property running into the thousands. The Specials provided the soundtrack with their magnificent "Ghost Town". Meanwhile the rest of the world went crazy as Charles Windsor married Diana Spencer. I was much more interested in events which were unfolding at Headingley in Leeds. My childhood love of cricket returned as Ian Botham and Bob Willis put the Aussies to the sword as England came from nowhere to win the Ashes. At Old Trafford Botham hammered the Aussie bowlers to all corners of the ground in an awesome display of big hitting under leaden skies one memorable Saturday afternoon.

City were only a couple of players short of winning the championship. How many times had I said this over the years? But it seemed that John Bond held a similar opinion. He went out and bought Martin O'Neill from Norwich City before completing negotiations with Brian Clough at Forest a couple of weeks later to sign the great Trevor Francis. Anticipation was sky high as we made the short journey down to the Potteries for Francis's debut on the Fifth of September. The sky was blue, the sun shone brightly as outside the ground there seemed to be more City fans than Stoke. As we took up our places on the terraces behind the goal I looked out on a pitch that had never been greener and felt a rare surge of optimism as the suited City players emerged from the tunnel. All eyes settled on Trevor Francis. Could this really be the start of something? The Match programme included an article by Stoke Manager Richie Barker in which he praised the advent of the new three points for a win system which he believed would encourage attacking play. There was a bizarre interview with Trevor Francis which was clearly conducted some weeks ago as he talked about his relationship with Brian Clough and looked forward to the new season with Forest! Of much more interest was the controversy expressed over Coventry City's decision to introduce the first all-seater stadium in a bid to combat hooliganism. Suddenly there was a huge roar as the teams took to the field. It was great to see former Blue Mike Doyle at the heart of the Stoke defence. He should still have been playing for us! Stoke also included future Blue Adrian Heath and Lee Chapman in their attack. For City Martin O'Neill replaced Steve Mackenzie on the right side of midfield and Francis, wearing the number nine shirt, partnered Kevin Reeves up front. If Trevor felt any pressure about his huge £1.2 million price tag then he did not show it. Every time he touched the ball the Blues roared him on and he crowned a great display by scoring two goals right in front of us with substitute Phil Boyer adding a third. I cannot recall being as thrilled about a City debut before or since. He looked unstoppable.

A huge crowd welcomed him to Maine Road the following week as the Blues scraped a draw against Southampton. Unfortunately this was followed by the first of Trevor's long injury lay-offs and it began to seem as if the result depended on his appearance in the team. Bond tried to improve the squad by the controversial signing of his son Kevin and the much applauded return to Maine Road of Asa Hartford. Francis's return in early November sent City on a great run as they won seven out of nine games. Dennis Tueart in particular hit a rich vein of form playing just off the front two and he hammered in six goals.

We were all dreaming of a White Christmas as only two fixtures were played on Boxing Day and City produced a rare win at Anfield. A couple of days later Wolves were the visitors to Maine Road. The afternoon was dark, icy rain began to fall and the surface was very greasy as kick off approached. The floodlights were on from the start as the teams took to the field. By now Gerry Gow had lost his ever present fight against injury and Martin O'Neill had disappeared from the line- up. He was only to make one further appearance in a strangely short City career. It seems strange that such a fine player who had so much success with Forest rarely got a look in at Maine Road. Nobody has ever really said why. Dennis Tueart had picked up a serious injury the week before Christmas so the side took on an unfamiliar look for the visit of Wolves. In front of Big Joe the back four consisted of Ray Ranson, Nicky Reid, Tommy Caton and Kevin Bond. In midfield Asa Hartford and Tommy Hutchison were flanked by youngsters Steve Kinsey and debutant Clive Wilson, with Francis and Reeves up front. In one of those typical City home games the Blues had all the play but conceded a sloppy goal and with minutes to go it looked like we were going to have to settle for a point and miss out on the chance of going top of the League. Just when we had all but given up Trevor Francis picked up the ball just inside the Wolves half and unleashed an unstoppable shot from fully fifty yards, or so it seemed. The ball flew past the helpless keeper and nearly took the netting off the goal at the Platt Lane End. Cue absolute pandemonium in the Kippax. Macker grabbed hold of me as we tumbled down the steps towards the pitch. I took a left hook from Phil as my glasses flew into the air. It was all we could do to keep on our feet. We regained our places and I groped around on the floor to retrieve my "specs". Fortunately I managed to get them but they were a lens missing! Nothing though could spoil the feeling as the referee blew his whistle. City were top of the League!! The rain sheeted down as we left the Kippax and we were floating on air as we reached the car. In the kingdom of the blind the one eyed man is king, so they say. I was the driver so despite the pouring rain I found it easiest to simply close one eye and set off in the general direction of home.

SIX.

PALE BLUES.

I was having a bite to eat in Lewis's café on Market Street when the general hubbub was pierced by high pitched screaming. A table was knocked over with plates, food and cutlery everywhere as a young man in his early twenties was writhing around on the floor holding his ears and screaming for dear life. Order was restored and people resumed their conversations. He was led away by the waitress who whispered almost apologetically to the onlookers that "He was in the Falklands, you know."

April brought the Falklands war on to our T.V. screens every night. British shores were lined with tearful sweethearts and inconsolable yet proud mothers as ships laden with troops set off for the South Atlantic. Daily broadcasts were given by a government official on the News and places such as South Georgia, Port Stanley, and Goose Green became depressingly familiar. Images seemed mainly to consist of barren windswept farmland as far as the eye could see, and lines of Argentinian prisoners stretching to the horizon. The Sun newspaper trumpeted the deeds of "our boys" in their own inimitable style and Prime Minister Margaret Thatcher revelled in the glory and ultimate victory which arrived three months later.

As the New Year opened City were sitting pretty at the top of the League. But hindsight revealed that Trevor Francis's match-winning goal against Wolves marked another depressingly familiar false dawn. The Blues were punching above their weight and a couple of injuries revealed the squad to be threadbare. John Bond had given us all hope with a Wembley final, a season of swashbuckling football in the "City style", and especially the marquee signing of Francis. But the damage done by Malcolm Allison and his board of directors in the previous two years was irreversible. Of Bond's three key signings two, Gow and Hutchison, for reasons of age and injury were only to be short term gap fillers however great their individual ability. Martin O'Neill played only twelve games and outstanding youngsters Dave Bennett and Steve Mackenzie were mysteriously allowed to leave. The Blues limped out of both Cups in Round Four and the side which travelled to Old Trafford on the 27th of February contained the likes of teenage debutant Gary Jackson, ageing utility player John Ryan, and Scandinavian unknown Aage Hareide. I have rarely witnessed such a one-sided derby. Yet incredibly we came away with a point in a one-all draw. We literally had only one attack in the whole game. Ray Ranson scampered down the right wing shrugging off a couple of weak tackles before delivering a superb cross to the near post where Kevin Reeves glanced it past the keeper. The Scoreboard End erupted packed as it was with Blues. In the Stretford Paddock surrounded by Reds I thrust my hands as far as I could into my pockets and shrugged sheepishly at the bloke next to me while bursting inside with joy. Joe Corrigan kept the Reds at bay practically on his own for the rest of the afternoon and like me he was probably relieved to hear the final whistle.

City were to win only five games out of twenty as the season ended on a flat note despite the reasonable finish of tenth place. One of those victories was on the tenth of March at Elland Road the home of old foes Leeds United. It was a bitterly cold Wednesday night yet I decided to drive across the Pennines myself and asked if any of the lads in the pub fancied it. A tumbleweed blew slowly through the vault of The Lancashire Fold in Middleton as everybody looked at their shoes. There was nothing else for it. I decided to go straight from work. As I hit the top of the M62 a gentle sleet started to fall and as I emerged from the car an icy wind bit into my face. The City following that night was the lowest that I can remember at Leeds. Indeed the attendance was only 20797, which was an indication of the hard times that Leeds too had fallen on.

The edge and electric atmosphere from previous meetings was markedly absent. As in previous seasons I took up a place in the paddock alongside the pitch with the sparse City following to my left. That night the two sides could hardly string two passes together and shots on goal were a rarity. Kevin Reeves popped up with the only goal of the game, snow began to fall and the ground quickly emptied. The Leeds fans grumbled and groaned as they approached the exits but curiously seemed to accept their fate. Despite the poor performance I was thrilled with the victory. On the way back all thoughts of football soon disappeared as I gripped the steering wheel tightly and peered through the windscreen as heavy snow began to fall. I was somewhere near the spot where the M62 splits to avoid the farmhouse in the middle when the unthinkable happened. The car simply conked out at seventy miles an hour and skidded to a halt in the fast lane. Luckily for me there was nobody immediately behind me and eventually the knights of the Automobile Association arrived and sent me back on my way. I arrived home in the early hours to the sound of my mum whispering "You are a bit late, aren't you son? I was starting to get a bit worried." Not as much as me, mum, I thought, as I soon drifted off into a fitful sleep.

At times like this it is difficult to pin down what actually drove me to follow such "Pale Blues" around the country watching matches which held no real significance. Nevertheless two weeks later in bright sunshine I headed off up the A1 to Middlesborough for a Division One fixture which attracted a crowd of only 11709. I arrived in good time to wander around Ayresome Park which reminded me very much of Maine Road with its rows and rows of terrace houses and back entries with fresh piles of manure courtesy of the huge police horses stationed on every corner. I must say that despite the lovely weather and low key fixture the local teenagers seemed to be "eyeing me up" as an away fan and I felt a definite chill in the air. I decided to try and buy a ticket for the main stand seats which seemed to be on open sale. This I did and entered the turnstiles and bought the customary programme. I looked at my watch. It was only twenty to two. There was hardly a soul in the ground. As kick off approached the ground just did not fill up. There were rows of empty seats all around and the few City fans that were present were in a small segregated pen by the corner flag in the far corner. What a huge contrast to the packed terraces in the tension filled League Cup semi final only five years earlier. As the teams were read out I barely recognised the City team. At least Big Joe was in goal. There was a back four of Ray Ranson, Nicky Reid, Tommy Caton and Clive Wilson. But the midfield was the most inexperienced that I can ever remember consisting of Steve Kinsey, Aage Hareide, Gary Jackson and Andy Elliott making his one and only appearance for the side. Hareide was a centre half, Kinsey a striker and I did not know what position Elliott played. Having watched the game I am none the wiser. Usual strikers Kevin Reeves and Trevor Francis hardly had any service and I cannot remember such a game where we hardly had a shot at goal. Francis must have wondered what he was doing in a team like this. He had recently played in the European Cup Final for Forest and scored the winning goal! The Boro game was played out like an end of season testimonial and both sides were "lucky to get nil"! When I walked into the Lancashire Fold pub I felt a strange surge of pride that I was one of the few who had supported the Blues on that day, but my friends just gave me strange looks and carried on with their conversations.

The Easter programme confirmed my worst suspicions. A healthy crowd of 40112 welcomed the mighty Liverpool to Maine Road. Francis was again out injured to be replaced by the lightweight Kinsey up front. I am sure Kinsey played with a comb in his back pocket but he made few waves against a Liverpool defence ably marshalled by a bearded Mark Lawrenson and "Pinocchio" Phil Thompson. The Kippax was tightly packed and the bus drivers were in good voice behind us. In fact the atmosphere was as it usually was when the scousers came to town. There was more than a hint of violence in the air both on and off the field. The tension soon lifted when it became apparent that as a game it was no contest. Sammy Lee hammered the first after only eight minutes and the game was over as Phil Neal added a penalty at the Platt Lane end before half time. After the break Liverpool were rampant as Craig Johnston scored a tap in, Alan Kennedy a screamer and finally Ian Rush made it five-nil to the Reds. I did not want to remind the lads that City had had first shout on Rush when he was a teenager at Chester. Hardly a word was spoken as Phil, Macker and I made our way back to the car. "What about Monday?" asked Macker. "Are we still going to Wolves?"

On Easter Monday we duly made the trip down to Wolverhampton where we sat on the front row in the new stand surrounded by a couple of thousand Blues. The sun was again shining and I really fancied this one. Trevor was pronounced fit and I figured that our three pronged attack of Reeves, Francis and Kinsey would run them ragged. Thirty minutes into the game we were four goals down. That was nine in the last two hours of football! How much more were we supposed to take? Bobby McDonald scored the only goal of the second half to give the score some respectability. But what on earth was happening? We were top of the League three months earlier. I was absolutely relieved when the season ended that we had stacked up so many points in the first half of the season otherwise we would surely have been relegated.

Like City I had certainly reached a crossroads by the summer of 1982 and felt that something had to change. Five years earlier I had been happy to take a job which would fund my nights out with the lads in the night clubs and bars of Manchester that Police Chief James Anderton had not managed to close down. As long as I had enough money to pay for a fortnights holiday in Majorca or Rimini and still have enough for my Kippax

Season Ticket then that would do me. But working in an office was slowly killing me and I had to find something else. And I did not have to look too far for inspiration. My dad and brother Pete were both teachers, and younger brother Paul and best mate Macker were both training for the world's second oldest profession. One night when we were all sat round watching "Coronation Street" dad asked me "Have you done anything about applying for Teacher Training?" "Not really, dad, no." I grunted in reply. It is funny how often a simple sentence in isolation can have such a profound effect on the rest of somebody's life. It was as if a light had switched on and a load removed from my shoulders. Without saying anything to anybody I started looking into getting into teaching and managed to secure myself an interview at the local Catholic Teacher Training College. Almost comically I was simultaneously promoted at work and summoned down to the Head Office in Manchester to be congratulated by the Big Chief. This meeting was scheduled for the same morning as I was due to attend my interview at college. So I went through the motions of pretending to be ever so grateful and delighted to be looking forward to such a rewarding career in banking before racing across town to make my eleven o'clock interview at college. The Principal was pretty pleased with my answers and I felt that I was doing fine until he asked me what subject I intended to teach. I had not even given it a thought. I mean it had just not occurred to me that I had to teach "something". He could see that I was floundering and helped me by asking what I had been good at at school. Without a moment's hesitation I settled on French. That was it then. I was in! I was floating on air as I returned to work and immediately handed in my notice. With my promotion at least my last month's salary would be slightly more than usual. My mum was devastated that I had given up such a "good" job in such a carefree manner. But I was ecstatic.

All it needed now to make my world complete was for the Blues to sign three or four high quality Division One regulars to help push us up the table and challenge for a trophy or two. But everything in the garden was not so rosy at Maine Road. In fact the club was almost bankrupt. The million pound signings and sky high wages of the last few years had pushed the club to the brink. The most obvious solution was the one that the fans could not contemplate. Peter Swales promptly sold the magnificent Trevor Francis to Sampdoria in Italy claiming that City could not afford him. With him went all hope of challenging for honours, but also the realisation dawned that City did not have the means to do so. As the Jam sang this was the bitterest pill which was too hard to swallow for some. Thousands of supporters walked away from the club at this point. Forty two thousand fans watched Francis's home debut twelve months earlier but only twenty seven thousand would attend the first home game without him when the season opened. Letters of protest and returned season tickets poured in as fans vented their fury on the selling of Francis. Plans to develop Maine Road and join up the stands had to be scrapped as economy measures took a hold. In order to appease the fans Bond bought the much travelled striker David Cross and Southampton midfielder Graham Baker. Both were hard working players but their signings were a clear indication to the supporters of where the club was pitching its sights. Local boy Cross from Heywood was a goal scoring journey man who every two years or so managed to get himself a new club no doubt taking a lucrative cut of any transfer fee. Nobody could really blame him for that. Graham Baker was simply a trier and was very soon christened "Hilda" by some of the fans.

Amazingly the season began with three straight victories, the most memorable being the single goal win over Elton John's Watford at Maine Road. The Blues for the first time in their history wore shirts with the sponsor's name of SAAB emblazoned across their chests. The game was also significant in that they lost keeper Corrigan to injury after only a few minutes play. Left back Bobby McDonald took over as there were no substitute goalies in those days. Watford threw the kitchen sink at him but he turned in an inspired performance as Tueart scored and the Blues hung on for a famous victory. Joe's injury was to keep him out for a few weeks and it was good to see young Alex Williams getting a run in the side. He certainly did not let anybody down. Striker Chris Jones signed from Spurs and played three games in the autumn before disappearing from the squad altogether and the Blues turned to sixteen year old young winger Paul Simpson against Coventry at Maine Road.

On the 23rd of October I made my annual pilgrimage to Old Trafford with more than the usual trepidation for the derby match. United were top of the table after ten games and City were in eighth place. Phil and I stood in the Stretford Paddock for this one as you could still buy tickets on open sale right up to the day of the game. So much for United's acclaimed support. The programme rather patronisingly indicated that "City now confidently believe in a successful bid for the League championship" and "we would have the exciting prospect of United and City being the two chief contenders for the League championship". This was Ron Atkinson's United which on paper did look a very good side. They had Gary Bailey in goal with Moran and McQueen in the centre of defence. A formidable midfield included Ray Wilkins, Bryan Robson, Arnold Muhren and Steve Coppell with Norman Whiteside and Frank Stapleton up front. City put out their most experienced side for this one and I reckon that there were about ten thousand Blues in a crowd of 57334. Yet the whole experience of travelling to the match and walking around the stadium filled me with dread on every visit. But I just had to be there, and was even prepared to spend the whole afternoon surrounded by Reds in complete silence. This was particularly difficult on this occasion as City gave it everything to repel the Red attacks and even raced into a two goal lead courtesy of a Tueart header and a David Cross tap in at the Stretford End. Even two was not enough at Old Trafford and when Frank Stapleton pulled one back you just knew that we would not be able to hang on. Frank duly supplied an equaliser but at least we managed to salvage a point.

A week before Christmas Dave Lamb invited myself, Phil and Macker over to Padgate College near Warrington for the end of term ball. As the grey of the afternoon turned to black and the snow began to fall the M62 became an ice rink. We certainly needed a drink when we arrived and Padgate College did not disappoint! The D.J. was none other than the great John Peel and Dave seemed to be on first name terms with him. Peel duly introduced a new young band from Liverpool to the assembled throng. Leather clad and flanked by glamorous go-go dancers they turned in a really powerful aggressive set which blew everybody away. Months later they got rid of the dancing girls and turned up on "Top of the Pops" as Frankie Goes To Hollywood. I suppose it has a better ring to it than "Frankie goes to Padgate".

By now Liverpool were five points clear of United at the top of the table while City could be relatively pleased with their position of ninth. Dave Lamb announced that he could get hold of tickets for the game at Anfield on the 27th of December. I had not been to Anfield for years but was pleased to learn that they now had seats in the Anfield Road End. Dave said that he would pick me up in his Orange Volkswagon Beetle at nine o' clock for a half eleven kick off for this holiday fixture. By ten he had not turned up and I was pacing up and down in my front room. There was no answer on his phone. I decided to bite the bullet and ran around to his house to find him on his drive revving up his obviously flat battery. He mumbled his apologies and we raced back to my house and off we went in my trusty Mazda! Conditions were again poor on the M62 and Dave stammered that he did not have the tickets but we were supposed to be meeting a mate of his from college who would have the said items. I looked at my watch. It was already a quarter past eleven and we were still some ten miles outside Liverpool. The day was certainly turning into a disaster. I thought that Dave's mate would have given us up and surely gone through the turnstiles without us. Yet as we ran around the corner of a deserted Anfield Road there he was kicking his heels against the kerb no doubt cursing Lammy and the fact that he had missed three of his beloved Liverpool's goals all scored by the great Kenny Dalglish. Although we had only missed a quarter of an hour City were three goals down already as we entered the ground and took up our seats in the Liverpool section. A massacre was in the offing. This was the great Liverpool side of Grobbelaar, Lawrenson, Whelan, Hansen, Souness, Rush and Dalglish. The game as a contest was over but our entry into the ground must have inspired City as they began to mount a few attacks. Indeed Lammy and I witnessed a two all draw with City goals coming from Tommy Caton and David Cross. Unfortunately the score in the paper next day confirmed a Liverpool victory by five goals to two. We stopped off on the way home for a couple of pints and I had time to have a look at the Match programme. An interesting article on City referred to a number of players who the Blues were trying to sign. But significantly it added that they were all either loans or player exchanges. Players mentioned included Frank Worthington, Peter Barnes, Stan Cummins and Justin Fashanu. The next page added that Trevor Francis had only played three games for Sampdoria before falling once more to injury.

At the beginning of the Eighties my teenage devotion to the Beatles had long been over and the death of John Lennon finally put paid to the constant rumours that they would reform. The Who had announced their farewell tour, The Stones had "gone disco" and even Seventies favourites Roxy Music called it a day in 1982. I had expected so much from punk rock in 1976, but I guess that its very nature ensured that it was short-lived. The solution to my search for something new and inspirational came from a totally unexpected source. On the Sixth of January 1983 I truly had a musical Epiphany! My girlfriend asked strangely if I fancied a night out with herself and her girlfriends from work. Normally I would run a mile from such an invitation as I have always found a group of girls far more intimidating than a group of boys. She mentioned that they were going into town to see a band called Foreign Press in a bar called the Manhattan Sound just off Portland Street. It was a bitterly cold evening as I walked down the narrow steps into the tiny basement club. Our group chose a couple of tables against the back wall with the bar to our right. The small dance floor was at the other end of the room where the band's amplifiers and drums were set up. I do not remember anything about Foreign Press or even if we saw them play that night. But the support band was phenomenal! There could only have been thirty or forty people in when they emerged from the back into the dimly lit room. I was delighted to see that there were no drum machines or synthesizer keyboards. This was a traditional four piece guitar band. There was also a manic male dancer who stood to the right of the lead singer. But it was the singer who immediately drew my attention. He was leaping around in a strangely uncoordinated way as Tony Wilson entered the room. "There's that guy off Granada Reports" said one of the girls as she downed her vodka and orange. The lead guitarist was playing as if his life depended on it and the bass and drums were really tight. I could not take my eyes off the lead singer as he strangely crooned his way through each rousing number ending with a squeal of absolute delight. His long angular face was joyfully contorted as he threw his arms around as if trying to embrace each and every one of us. Or so it seemed. He reached into his back pocket and showered us with confetti as he left the stage with a final whoop of delight! The guy behind the bar informed me that the band was called the Smiths and the singer liked to be known as Morrissey. When they made their debut on

Top Of The Pops a few weeks later I was thrilled to recognise them. The Manhattan was only the second gig that the Smiths had played. I have read since that hundreds were supposed to have been there. This was not the case.

Home crowds had dropped to around twenty two thousand by the time Norwich arrived at Maine Road on the fifteenth of January. New signing Peter Bodak had a fine game on the wing, David Cross provided a couple of excellent finishes and the Blues romped home by four goals to one. The next Saturday Phil and I travelled down to Villa Park in my Mazda and got great seats right behind the dugout on the half way line. Paul Power filled in at left back and Steve Kinsey returned to the line-up on the left. It was a fine open game of good attacking football with City wearing their change strip of red and black. Villa opened the scoring but Asa Hartford finished off a fine flowing move to earn us a point. We left the stand as soon as the whistle blew, strolled to our car and in no time were going back down the M6 at a rate of knots! The journey was a good one and in no time at all we pulled into the car park of The Swan at Knutsford. We walked into the lounge and I checked my watch. Bang on six o'clock. I was amazed to see Asa Hartford sat at the bar on his own sipping a pint of Lager! How had he managed to leave the pitch, shower and get changed and be back in the pub before us? We gathered our pints, took up our seats and began to cheerfully discuss our prospects for the rest of the season. We were handily placed in the top half of the table and were looking forward to a good run in the F.A. Cup. But being City, the wheels were about to come off.

The following week City surrendered tamely away at Brighton in the Cup losing by four goals to nil. Manager John Bond resigned that same evening claiming much later that he had been unhappy for some time and that he never felt that he had the total support of a number of Directors. Chairman Peter Swales quickly appointed assistant John Benson and that basically was that. There were only three victories from the next sixteen games and heavy defeats at Coventry, Swansea, Southampton and Liverpool. The magnificent Joe Corrigan was allowed to leave for America at the end of March and the players seemed to be just playing out the season. With each defeat City slid closer and closer to the abyss without actually falling into the relegation zone. In fact the final game of the season at home to Luton Town boiled down to City needing a point to avoid the big drop at the expense of their opponents that day.

There was huge interest in the fixture. We met in the Smith's Arms leaving Macker's brother Peter in the car as usual. Dave Lamb joined us for this one and there was a high level of excitement as we walked along the back of the North Stand towards the Kippax. Luton did not have a big following yet we did notice one or two orange and navy scarves on the corner by the ticket office. I glanced towards the main entrance just to make sure that the T.V. cameras were here. The presence of the huge vans confirmed this. We entered the stand via the tunnel slightly to the right of the centre circle. It was only half past two but already the Kippax was beginning to fill up. The usual faces were around us including Big Ted and the bus drivers. But it was clear that people were attending who had not been down to Maine Road for some time. One or two complained about the size of the fences around the ground which were now a regular feature at First Division grounds. There was even a fence in front of the Platt Lane Stand where most children including myself got their first taste of following the Blues and which had previously housed the Junior Blues. The official attendance was given as 42843 which was nineteen thousand up on the previous home game. City lined up crucially without leading scorer David Cross who had scored twelve goals in his only season in City colours. Alex Williams was in goal as usual with an experienced back four of Ranson, McDonald, Bond and Caton. Reid, Baker, Hartford and Power made up the midfield with Reeves and Tueart up front. On paper this was a strong line up and one which should never have been fighting for their lives. Luton needed to win in order to stay up and contained some useful attackers in their line up including the brilliant Paul Walsh who later moved on to Liverpool and of course to City. Their midfield warrior and captain was none other than Brian Horton who went on to become a popular manager of the Blues in the Nineties. He was just the sort of player that City needed that day. He chased everything and flung himself into the tackle. The atmosphere was highly charged and without a meaningful shot on goal the two teams left the pitch at half time. Nearly there! Macker removed and devoured two tangerines from his pocket before going down to the front to reassure brother Pete that everything was going to be all right. It did seem that City were trying to hold onto what they started with. A very dangerous strategy and not one that City usually adopted. The second half passed in a blur. There seemed to be no real danger of losing but my stomach was in absolute knots. I looked at my watch. Twenty five to five. There could only be minutes left. Attacks became increasingly frantic and there was a strange hush around the ground as the ball broke to Luton substitute Raddy Antic who let fly from the edge of the area. The ball seemed to take a deflection off a City leg before flying up into the roof of the net beyond the grasp of Alex Williams. A goal down with only minutes left. I looked around at largely stunned faces. One or two began to swear vociferously at individual players. There were tears in some eyes. The final whistle went. Some players slumped to their knees. Others ran from the pitch as quickly as they could. Luton Manager David Pleat ran across towards us in the Kippax with his arms raised in triumph to embrace Brian Horton. Children started to cry and some fans began to scale the fences in an attempt to get on the field. Police and stewards were slow to react as one or two "supporters" moved towards the players. For a few moments things looked a little ugly but thankfully players on both sides managed to get off the pitch safely. I felt numb. We were down.

SEVEN.

TERRACE APART, AGAIN.

Teacher training college was a real shock to the system! There were only twelve hours of lectures a week! The lecturers were mainly in their fifties and seemed to be living the life of Riley. They seemed to know instinctively that they were onto a good thing. I struggled with all my early essays and seemed far too earnest compared to my classmates who were all eighteen and had only just left school! Where I treated college like a "proper" job and put the hours in in the library they spent most of their time in bed or in the bar! Although I was only five years older the gulf seemed vast and it did not help that I lived off campus in the real world in a flat in Salford 7. The flat did not have a telephone and I had to wander over to a public phone box outside the Kersal pub nearby to organise lifts to the match and arrange my regular Tuesday night rendezvous with Macker. Although we had both left Middleton (Macker had a room in a large house in Didsbury) we were determined to meet up at least once a week to discuss the fortunes of the Blues over a few pints of Boddies.

The last time City were in Division Two they were led by Joe Mercer and Malcolm Allison and they swept all before them with a swashbuckling side that included Tony Book, Glyn Pardoe, Colin Bell, Mike Summerbee, Mike Doyle and Neil Young. They achieved promotion in 1966 at the height of Beatlemania on a tidal wave of euphoria. "Joe Mercer came, we played the game, we went to Rotherham....." In the summer of 1983 John Benson was shown the door to be replaced by the Celtic great Billy McNeill. Jimmy Frizzell from Oldham was appointed as his assistant but even the most diehard City fan doubted that the Blues had what it takes to do a "Joe and Mal" and achieve promotion. McNeill did himself no favours by making his thoughts public that City contained "eight" good players in their ranks. I am not sure that this was a good idea. I guess that the "eight" that he was referring to was what was left of the squad in Alex Williams, Ray Ranson, Nicky Reid, Kevin Bond, Tommy Caton, Paul Power, Asa Hartford and Graham Baker. Bobby McDonald had been sensationally sacked for "driving offences" and Tueart and Reeves were deemed too expensive to keep on. It did not take a genius to work out that we did not have an experienced striker at the club and moreover that eleven players constituted a football team. Strikers Derek Parlane and Jim Tolmie were plucked cheaply from Scottish football but McNeill's masterstroke was surely the £30000 paid in securing the services of Neil McNab from Brighton. Youngster Andy May completed the line-up by slotting into the left back position even though he was predominantly right footed.

City began well by winning eight of the first eleven fixtures with home crowds holding up at 25000. These victories included the demolition of Blackburn Rovers on the Seventeenth of September with a hat trick from the slick Parlane and a thunderbolt from winger Tolmie whose moustache and permed hair marked him out as a real Eighties man! The programme that day reminded us that the Football League was sponsored for the first time in its history by camera manufacturers Canon. The Souvenir Shop alongside the ground sold Home Shirts for £9.95 and Baby Doll nightwear for £4.99! A SAAB 900 Turbo had "more power than Paul" and a sixteen year old Earl Barrett signed YTS forms with the club bemoaning the fact that they had to pay him £25 a week.

The Blues were to suffer a reality check when on the 29th of October we suffered a five-nil defeat to a Kevin Keegan inspired Newcastle United. The Geordies also included Peter Beardsley and Chris Waddle in their ranks. Although the nature of the defeat surprised many including myself, this did not stop me taking a train down to Shrewsbury the following Saturday. The tension of the cup defeat at Gay Meadow four years earlier was conspicuous by its absence. It was a bright crisp autumn day as the teams took to the field and I was pleased to have a seat in the City section in the Main Stand with the majority of our support behind the goal to my right still behind huge fences. Steve Kinsey was brought in for his first full game of the season to partner Parlane in attack with Paul Power and Jim Tolmie providing support on the wings. But it was the wily McNab who was controlling the game in midfield. Shrewsbury had no answer to City's slick football and we ran out easy winners by three goals to one with Andy May, Tommy Caton and Steve Kinsey getting on the scoresheet. The man in the boat by the river did not need to get his boots wet as City played slick football on the deck.

It was becoming clear that the big four of Chelsea, Newcastle, Sheffield Wednesday and City were going to be contesting the three promotion places and a narrow victory at Stamford Bridge was followed by a home defeat to Wednesday before a huge crowd of 41852. Unfortunately young Tommy Caton who had made his debut at the age of sixteen for the Blues and who was certainly a prospective England International chose this important pre- Christmas period to rock the boat by handing in a transfer request. I felt a deep sense of betrayal and did not understand why he wanted to leave City at this point to ply his trade in the First Division. Why could he not wait a few months like the rest of us? After all, none of us liked being in the Second Division playing the likes of Cambridge, Carlisle and Grimsby. Caton duly got his dream move to Arsenal but he had not done his homework. The Gunners already contained a highly promising centre back who was to go on and make hundreds of appearances for Arsenal and become a mainstay of the England defence. None other than Tony Adams! Consequently Caton's career at Highbury was short-lived and he did not really fulfil his early promise. Shortly afterwards McNeill signed a more than able replacement in Barnsley Captain Mick McCarthy who had performed so well at Maine Road earlier in the season.

I took it for granted that I had been able to follow City around the country for years by car, coach and train. I had learnt back at school in Russian lessons that this was not the case in other parts of the world where freedom to travel was prohibited. This state of affairs soon began to be played out in Margaret Thatcher's Britain in 1984. As the Miner's Strike developed and pickets travelled to pits around the country Thatcher saw this as a personal challenge to her authority. The police were instructed to set up road blocks on the motorways to prevent people from travelling and Britain began to resemble a Police State. Violent battles between the miners and police filled our screens as mining communities were crushed and pits closed down. Phil and I took the service train to Barnsley deep in the heart of mining country for the away fixture just after Christmas. As the train pulled into Barnsley station Phil muttered "look at this, Tim". I looked out of the window to see hundreds of police, some in riot gear, with their snarling dogs stationed all along the platform. With the mist closing in around the weak station lights it seemed like a scene from Nazi Germany! This was not even a football train and the game was not due to start for some four hours! As the doors to the train opened the police asked all those getting off if they were going to the match. To be honest, most were not. They were mainly Saturday shoppers. Phil and I were not wearing any colours and shook our heads so as not to give away our Manchester accents. Some lads were manhandled into a station yard where I glimpsed hundreds of others crammed in against high walls and surrounded by huge horses and distinctly unfriendly Alsatian dogs. I presume that they would be held there for hours before being marched to the turnstiles. We looked straight ahead and without a backward glance headed for the exits and a reasonable pub between the station and the ground. I bet that some of those lads are still in that station yard to this day! It was absolutely freezing on the open terrace at Oakwell but the Blues returned with a well-earned point with a goal from Derek Parlane.

City were not pulling up any trees in the New Year. Indeed many clubs saw City as a real scalp in what was truly their "Cup Final". This was never more apparent than on March the 17th when I managed to persuade my Middleton pal Phil to make the long trip down to Fulham with me. We decided to go by train and met on a very cold platform on a windswept Piccadilly Station shortly after six o'clock. I could still taste the stale beer from the night before as I clumsily wrestled with a paper cup of British Rail tea. Phil chose to remain silent. He must have been cursing me for getting him here at this unearthly hour. It is a good job that he had no idea how the day would pan out! We boarded the train and muttered something that may have resembled conversation as the stations passed. Stockport…Macclesfield….Stoke-On-Trent…. We occasionally remarked on supporters of other teams as we noticed the occasional scarf or team badge. Fans were not as keen to show their allegiances in the mid-eighties. It was just too dangerous. Phil and I travelling incognito as usual were just starting to wake up around Birmingham New Street when I realised that today was the day of the Boat Race on the Thames. I had watched these epic tussles between Oxford and Cambridge every year on Grandstand and had noticed that the boats always went past Fulham football ground. What an opportunity to see it for ourselves!

We left the train at Euston, boarded the Tube and found ourselves at noon on Putney Bridge, pint in hand, awaiting the arrival of the boats. There was huge anticipation amongst the friendly mainly student crowd. We waited in vain. The boats did not arrive. This was the year when one of the boats sank immediately after the start! This was the first time that this had happened and we were there! We finished our drinks and as the crowds dispersed we made our way along the bank towards Craven Cottage. At least we still had the game to look forward to. We walked through the park spotting celebrity fans as we went.

"Is that Dennis Waterman over there?"

"There's Jimmy Hill by the hot dog stand". Fulham was such a friendly place. I had begun to get a real good feeling about this match. How wrong could I be? The friendly jovial crowd around us in the paddock was not matched by the Fulham gang behind the goal who taunted young Alex Williams throughout the first half with despicable monkey chants. Elsewhere on the field City did not get a kick. I was so pleased to see former idol Asa Hartford get a rare run out, but Fulham ran rings around us and led by five goals to nil after 46 minutes! Even Gordon Davies looked like a good player! What a nightmare! We pulled one back through Neil McNab but the journey home seemed like one of the longest in my life. Hardly a word was spoken. There were no taxis available at the station and as I staggered in the front door I looked at my watch. Half past one!

Neil McNab picked up an injury which was to keep him out for a few weeks as the Blues stuttered on the run-in. A visit from leaders Chelsea on a Friday night for live television attracted a crowd of only twenty one thousand. The general consensus in those pre-Sky days was that live football on television on Friday and Monday nights would eventually be played in empty stadiums which would lead to the end of the game as we knew it. There was also more than a hint of trouble in the air as it seemed that there were Chelsea fans in all four stands. On the pitch the Blues surrendered tamely losing by two goals to nil to a Chelsea side which included icons Kerry Dixon, David Speedie and Pat Nevin. I felt an incredible sense of emptiness at the final whistle. Perhaps due to the strange atmosphere in the ground, maybe the fact that it was played on a Friday night, but most probably because of the disappointment of finishing fourth place in the table. I tried to convince myself that it had not been that bad a season. After all, strikers Parlane and Tolmie had proved to be excellent value finishing with sixteen and thirteen goals respectively. There had been great performances from youngsters Alex Williams, Andy

May, Clive Wilson and Steve Kinsey. What is more, experienced campaigners Mick McCarthy and Neil McNab had been tremendous signings! I was sure that we would do it next time round.

As I looked at the faces of Phil and Macker, like most now shorn of their semi-moustaches so prevalent in the early Eighties, it was clear that they did not share my optimism! We talked long into the night in Corbieres to the strains of early Smiths singles like "Hand in Glove" and "This Charming Man", "Reward" by Teardrop Explodes and the "Killing Moon" by Echo and the Bunnymen. These tracks would compete on the jukebox with old favourites such as The Doors, Jimi Hendrix, James Brown and The Stones.

City started the new season as favourites for promotion. They made two major signings, David Phillips in midfield and the rather "hefty" Tony Cunningham up front. It was clear from day one that Cunningham was not really fitting into the side and he seemed to be on a different wavelength to the prolific Parlane. The Blues won only two of the first six games with Parlane scoring four goals and Cunningham failing to get off the mark. Incredibly City allowed Parlane to join Swansea on a free transfer and kept faith with Cunningham! Neil McNab began to be troubled by injuries and just when I was starting to fear the worst results took a turn for the better. The defence was as solid as ever with Williams performing his usual heroics behind a back four of Andy May, Nicky Reid, Mick McCarthy, and Paul Power. What was really pleasing was the way youngsters David Phillips and Clive Wilson were playing alongside "Hilda" Baker in midfield. Steve Kinsey, although very lightweight and often more concerned with keeping his hair in place, was beginning to fulfil his early potential and hit the target on a more regular basis. Another Scot Gordon Smith, who had been certain to score at Wembley against United in 83 for which crime some never forgave him, also began to chip in with a goal or two. The signing of Jim Melrose in November from Celtic sparked off a great run in which the Blues won four out of six with Melrose scoring in five consecutive matches. The goal he got against Notts County on December the 8th was worthy of a cup final as he turned and hammered home from fully forty yards. It is a pity that only 20109 were there to see it! The unfortunate Tony Cunningham even managed to score a goal but lost his place to Melrose and was sold soon after to Newcastle United. By Boxing Day City were up to fifth in the League and two days later put four past Wolves to ensure a happy Christmas at Maine Road.

All of a sudden in January Jim Melrose stopped scoring. Luckily David Phillips took up the mantle by scoring five in six matches! He specialised in thirty yard rockets and by the end of February City had risen to second in the table. On the 2nd March City travelled to Blackburn for a traditional six pointer at the top of the League. Macker drove us over the tops and I thought it a little strange when he pulled up outside a Catholic church on the outskirts. I know that he was a little worried about this game but I thought it was taking it a little too far by praying for the right result. Before I had time to protest he informed me that this was his Uncle Peter's Church. He was in fact the Parish Priest and Macker said he would call in as we were in the area. Nevertheless I still felt a little strange as we entered the hall of the presbytery. My nerves disappeared completely as we entered the lounge and I noticed the huge rug with a massive Manchester City crest on it! Father Peter was brought up in Moss Side and was a rabid Blue. After a quick sandwich and coffee we said our goodbyes and were soon walking down the hill to Ewood Park with huge optimism. With God on our side how could we go wrong? The queues for the City end were huge so we decided to try the paddock which ran alongside the pitch. I had been locked out of Anfield in the Seventies and so it was with huge relief that we managed to get into the ground by ten to three. We were surrounded by middle aged

Rovers fans who were more concerned with eating their pies than causing any trouble. I was pleased to see the Blues were wearing their red and black second strip which always took me back to the 69 Cup Final. The first twenty minutes were all Blackburn and local hero Simon Garner went close on a couple of occasions. Nicky Reid and Mick McCarthy were outstanding and Paul Power started to make several probing runs down the left. It was from one of these runs and crosses that Steve Kinsey managed to scuff in our winner in the goal to our right. Macker inadvertently threw his half time tangerine peels into the air in delight which did not go down too well with the locals. But there were City fans all over the place and tangerines apart we did not stand out. City managed to hang on as Blackburn mounted a few late attacks and at last the final whistle blew. For the first time that season City were top of the league. The fixture list looked kind. We were as good as there. As we walked up the Darwen Road back to the car the City supporters began to take up the Culture Club song "Karma karma, karma karma, karma Cham-e-leon, we're going up, we're going up….."

A couple of routine home victories followed but the injuries were beginning to pile up. Graham Baker dislocated his shoulder in the victory over Blackburn soon to be followed by a lengthy absence for the influential McNab. Reinforcements came in with the re-signing of old favourite Kenny Clements from Oldham Athletic and the inexperienced full back Geoff Lomax was plucked from the reserves, with Andy May being pushed forward into midfield. The Blues dropped to fifth after three draws and heavy defeats at Oxford and Grimsby. With the squad down to its bare bones former child prodigy (he played for the first team at sixteen) Paul Simpson was recalled from a loan spell in Ireland and he not only chipped in with a few goals but he also gave the side real impetus going forward. The Blues clung to the third promotion place with two games to go. Amazingly, or maybe not, after so many false dawns, none of the lads fancied the trip down to Meadow Lane for the Bank holiday fixture with Notts County where a win would guarantee promotion. It was a case of don't look now, here comes Keogh with that "anyone fancy going to the next away game" look on his face. I asked around and eventually managed to cadge a lift off a friend of my brother who was more at home on the golf course but a real City fan.

As we made our way nervously along the M1 it seemed that every passing car, coach or van was sporting City colours. Meadow Lane was only a stones throw from the Notts Forest ground and we managed to park up in a side street not unlike those around Maine Road. The area around the turnstiles was absolutely jammed packed with the stewards and police struggling to keep order. There did seem to be an unusually high proportion of "day trippers" who had clearly drunk Nottingham dry and were not in the mood for any messing about. A photograph taken of the City end which appeared on the cover of the following week's programme showed not only how packed it was, but perhaps significantly how the following appeared to be entirely male apart from one or two families at the front peering through the fence. City seemed to have been allocated at least three quarters of what was a really ramshackle ground with County fans mainly dotted around the main stand area. In the spring sunshine the pitch was really bare and heavily sanded reminding me of the Baseball Ground up the road in nearby Derby. There was real tension in the air due mainly to the huge expectation from the mass ranks of Blues. If will alone was enough then City would have sailed through into the First Division. The team contained five full backs in Clements, Power, Lomax, Reid and May with only the lightweight Steve Kinsey and Paul Simpson up front. Notts County in their famous black and white stripes had no intention of rolling over to the mighty Blues. In fact their players sensed the occasion and were really up for it. Their tactics seemed to be brutally simple. They clattered into City's lightweight side at every opportunity and kicked the ball as hard and as far as they could up the pitch. Most of the City youngsters froze but the formidable Mick McCarthy seemed to relish the battle and appeared to be taking them on on his own. Behind him young Alex Williams was at his best keeping the Blues in the game for as long as he could. It was one-way traffic from the first minute. Even with a team of full backs we were exposed on both flanks and a stream of crosses was flooding into the box. The ground became silent as the goals began to fly into the City net directly in front of us. Half time came. I was completely exhausted and could not believe what I was witnessing. Notts County 3 Manchester City 0! This was supposed to be our day. But to top everything off incredibly things soon began to get worse. Beer fuelled tensions and the inaction of the police and stewards led to some of the worst scenes that I have ever witnessed following the Blues. So-called "fans" began to rip down the huge perimeter fences and invade the pitch. Fights broke out all around the ground, with worst of all, some "fans" trying to make their way to the dressing room areas. Fortunately they did not succeed but it took a long time to restore order. The half time score was bad enough but watching these events unfold made me sick to the stomach. I was so proud to be a City fan and it is true that the worst excesses of football hooliganism had largely escaped us following the Blues home and away in the seventies and eighties. I was ashamed. I did not really care how the second half of the game went. The City fans who shamed the club that day were castigated in all the morning papers and manager Billy McNeill let his feelings be known in no uncertain terms in his programme notes the following week. Just for the record Simpson scored two goals in the second half as the Blues went down by three goals to two. But it hardly mattered. There were few words spoken in the car as the funeral procession inched its way out of Nottingham and up the motorway back home. If I was ever going to walk away from football it would have been that May night in 1985. But there must be something in my make-up, perhaps shared by thousands of Blues fans the world over, that refuses to give in, and believes that the next match will be "the one". They say that the darkest hour is right before the dawn and as far as I was concerned the dawn was to take place the next Saturday the 11th of May at Maine Road against Charlton Athletic. It was to be all or nothing!

The familiar butterflies were in my stomach as I awoke from a fitful sleep on the morning of the game. The facts were simple. All we had to do was win the match to join already promoted Oxford United and Birmingham City in the First Division. We were level on points with Portsmouth and had a five goal advantage which would surely be enough? The phone did not stop ringing all morning. It seemed that everybody was interested in this match. The Blues were crawling out of the woodwork to be at this one. Even brother Paul was coming over from Liverpool to join us in the Kippax! Macker had stocked up on his tangerines and his young brother Peter had plenty of reading material as we were joined by Phil in The Smith's Arms at an earlier than usual one o'clock. We clutched our pints to our chests as if our lives depended on it as we nervously discussed the possible line ups. Peter Gardner had revealed in The Evening News that City only had eleven fit players and that Mick McCarthy was suspended! As we left the pub the sun made a rare appearance over the huge Italian Church to our left. We parked up off Great Western Street making sure that we tipped our West Indian car minder (by now in his mid-twenties), and as I rounded the corner by the Souvenir Shop the concourse was a seething mass of sky blue and white! The Kippax car park was no different. The queues for the turnstiles were huge recalling the League Cup semi against Liverpool a few years earlier. We didn't get in until half time that night! But today we could use our season ticket vouchers and thankfully those queues were nowhere near as long. I bought a programme and we took up our place on the half way line. There was still half an hour to go as Macker produced his first tangerine. The programme told us that David Phillips had become the Junior Blues Player of The Year, that a young man called Ian Cheeseman from Chadderton had completed his travels to all 92 grounds of the Football League, and that spectators were requested to keep off the pitch at all times. I looked at the back of the programme. Alex Williams was in goal with a back four of Lomax, May, Clements and skipper Paul Power. David Phillips and Neil McNab anchored the midfield leaving the Blues with four up front consisting of the returning Melrose, Tolmie, Simpson and Kinsey. Charlton included a young Robert Lee who would later have a great career with Newcastle and future manager Alan Curbishley. I was delighted to note that their keeper had been plucked from the youth team only a week ago. Hopefully he would be a bag of nerves (like the rest of us).

As the teams took to the pitch the roar of the Kippax made the hairs stand up on the back of my neck. I could not remember such an ovation since Colin Bell made his comeback against Newcastle. The ground was so packed that you could not take your hands out of your pockets! There were people sat on the steps between the seats all around the ground, and some were even standing alongside the pitch all along the front of the Kippax! As the referee blew his whistle I looked around me. At best friends Macker and Phil who like me had witnessed too many disappointments, at young Peter with his nose pressed against the fence at the front and to brother Paul wearing his replica City shirt some fifteen years before everyone else followed suit! My thoughts turned momentarily to my granddad, now in his eighties, who had introduced me to all this back in 1966. Come on City! Do it for all these fantastic people!

The Blues hit Charlton with everything that they had got! The team and the crowd were as one. The sun shone as the goals rained in on Charlton's goal. Two blockbusters from David Phillips, a tap in for Paul Simpson and goals from Andy May and Jim Melrose completed a five-one rout. At the final whistle we all invaded the pitch. Before

I knew it I was stood on the penalty spot at the North Stand End having my picture taken. The players made it to the sanctuary of the dressing rooms as wild celebrations broke out all over the ground. We had done it!

Sadly the last day of the football season was marked by the terrible fire at Bradford City, to be closely followed by the tragedy at the Heysel stadium in which many Italian fans died after a stampede on the terraces at the European Cup final between Liverpool and Juventus. It seems incredible to think that we all watched helplessly as events unfolded on live television and even more unbelievable that the game then actually took place! Assuming that the players knew what had happened I am amazed that they could have taken to the field of play. Football was clearly in a perilous state. But even this was put into perspective by news reports about the biblical famine in Ethiopia. Cometh the hour, cometh the man. In July Bob Geldof revealed to the watching world that his heart was bigger than his mouth with his superb organisation of the Live Aid concert at Wembley. The bizarre attendance of Prince Charles and Lady Diana and the absence of Morrissey aside this was a tremendous occasion. Bono stole the show as he took to the cat walk and almost disappeared into the adoring crowds. The likes of Phil Collins and his egotistical transatlantic dash left me cold, but it was brilliant to see old troopers like Bowie, Jagger and Pete Townshend struttin' their stuff. Like everybody else I was devastated by the Cars' video, and I managed to stay up until four in the morning to see Bob Dylan struggle through a couple of numbers flanked by the clearly drunk Keith Richards and Ronnie Wood of The Rolling Stones. A flat end to a memorable day.

On the pitch with brother Paul after the Charlton game in 1985.

EIGHT.

FIRST CLASS.

September 1985 marked my first day as a teacher following my dad and brother Pete into the classroom. I had to struggle through a number of interviews before taking up a post in a tough area of Bolton. I did not help my cause much by mistaking the headteacher, who was dressed in an old green cardigan, for a gardener as I arrived for interview.

"Hey mate, can you tell me where the staff room is?" I cringed as moments later he appeared in his office surrounded by his governors who looked like extras off Father Ted. However I must have done something right as they gave me the job!

It was a long way to Bolton on public transport from North Manchester. I had to get the seven o'clock bus into Manchester before scampering across the city to Salford Bus station in order to catch the number eight to Bolton. When I got off the bus in Farnworth I still had half an hour's walk to the school gates. I relied on my trusty Walkman to pass the time on the journey. This caused me something of a dilemma as I much preferred buying LPs on vinyl but I took to buying some on cassette now for the daily bus journeys. One morning on the top deck I had to turn up the volume as two guys sitting directly behind me seemed to be planning an armed robbery as the bus rattled through Little Lever and Kearsley. At school the children were hard but friendly. They would offer you a crisp at break time but if the saw any sign of weakness then they took few prisoners. The staff was the salt of the earth and could not do enough to help in those first few difficult weeks. There were one or two exceptions. When I asked the Head of Religious Education what syllabus I was due to teach with my one class of Fifth Years he helpfully replied:

"Don't ask me. Do what you want". As I struggled to control this class of twenty eight boys and just two girls I asked the advice of one of the more helpful senior masters in the staffroom. The one with the tweed jacket with leather elbows, nicotine stained fingers and ever-present cup of coffee. He advised me to just dictate sentences to them and get the children to copy them down. Although deadly boring he reckoned that it was better to keep them busy than indulge in new ideas such as discussion and opinion! It actually worked but it was driving me round the bend. So after a couple of months I decided to try to get to know the lads, and the two lassies, of course. As I walked into the room the whole class were sat in silence with their pens clasped tightly in their hands hovering over their open exercise books in anticipation of the usual note-taking "slog".

"Did anybody see the match last night?" I enquired tentatively. There was no reply.

"Do you think it was a penalty?" I continued bravely. Still no reply, but several puzzled looks from the rows of blank faces. Suddenly the silence was broken from somewhere on the back row.

"Are we not doing sentences today, sir?"

There was a little fellow named Billy Hughes who sat right at the front with unkempt hair and a permanently puzzled look. I had been greatly influenced by Ken Loach's film "Kes" on my journey into teaching and here was the nearest thing to Billy Casper that I could ever imagine. Like his fictional counterpart Billy Hughes was tiny, stick thin, and looking years younger than the rest of his classmates. He was the only pupil in the school to wear a blazer. Unfortunately this marked him out from everybody else and like Billy Casper he was remorselessly bullied by most of his classmates, and according to him, by some of the teachers, too. It was clear that Billy could not cope with the reading and writing so as there was no such thing recognised as "special needs" in those days I decided to seek advice in the staff room.

"He likes colouring in", I was informed.

"Go down to Geography and get some of those printed black and white world maps and get him to colour the sea in blue and the land in green. He will love that." I followed this strange advice and Billy was perfectly happy each lesson with his map and green and blue pencil crayons. I was almost grateful as his shouts of "Sir, I have coloured the sea in green" punctuated the dull monotony of "sentences" lesson after lesson.

There was one particular day when this class really tested my mettle as a fledgling teacher and it involved little Billy. Sadly I had dispensed with my efforts to really engage the class and get them involved in discussions and had returned to the safer option of dictating notes. As I left the safety of my desk at the front and walked around the class as they slavishly copied down the sentences a tall gangly youth left his seat at the back, strode down to the front and promptly thumped Billy knocking him off his chair. After six months of things running pretty smoothly this was it! The big test and one which I had to pass.

"Come here, son," I thundered.

"What do you think that you are playing at?" I roared in the most authoritarian voice that I could muster. He walked over slowly and stood right in front of me. He was as tall as me and as he moved forward I could smell his dank breath on my face. "Leave the room immediately and get to the Headmaster's office!" I ordered. The class was deathly silent with all eyes on me as incredibly he took a step forward. He was visibly shaking as the words left his mouth.

"I am not going to do anything that you say, Keogh." The earth stood still. A tumbleweed blew through the classroom. The clock struck twelve. I was convinced that he was going to head butt me in front of all his friends. My legs were shaking. I could hardly breathe. After what seemed like an age but was probably only a few seconds the silence was broken by a dismembered voice from the back of the room.

"O.K. Pooley. You've really done it this time......" articulated Amanda Quinn before she resumed chewing her gum with great relief. Pooley immediately went bright red, burst into tears, and ran out of the door. Billy groaned as he got back in his seat and the pupils burst into a round of applause. Nobody really knew who it was for but at least I had stood my ground. The next lesson we resumed our dictation and winter turned into spring.

City were back in the First Division and were badly in need of reinforcements to boost a threadbare squad. Centre forward Mark Lillis, a self-confessed City fanatic was signed from Huddersfield and tried manfully to live the dream. The other major signing was the ex-United midfielder Sammy McIlroy who arrived with little fanfare from Stoke. I think it would be fair to say that he did not win over the fans. It was not because he did not have the charisma of Denis Law or Brian Kidd who had successfully crossed the divide before him. It was just that he seemed to be going through the motions. He even scored on his debut at Coventry but he made no real effort to win over the fans or to give himself totally to the City cause. These are essential qualities for City heroes. There were few tears shed for him as he made only fourteen appearances in the sky blue of City. The other signing of note was a centre half called Johnson from Rotherham with a trademark "Rob McCaffrey" style moustache who hardly played at all due to injury. On the few occasions that he took to the field it was clear that he was just too slow anyway. At the end of August The Blues beat Spurs at Maine Road in a close game which was unusual for the fact that City wore their Red and Black "away" shirts at home due to a clash of colours. Spurs must have forgotten to pack their awful yellow away strip that day!

Another significant change was the fact that away fans were now housed in the Platt Lane stand, formerly the home of the Junior Blues and where I watched my first matches with dad back in 1966. In a season of low attendances this had a negative influence on the atmosphere at matches. There were only a few hundred fans behind the goal except when teams like United, Liverpool or Everton provided the opposition.

After beating Spurs City did not win again for eleven matches and began to slip down the League table. Lillis and Paul Simpson chipped in with a few goals but clearly a striker of First Division quality was needed if City were to re-establish themselves in the top flight. Unfortunately Gordon Davies was signed from Chelsea. He was a finisher in the mould of Jimmy Greaves or Ian Rush. Yet he did not possess the ability of either. Keeper Alex Williams sustained a serious injury as the Blues surrendered tamely against United in September and did not play again for the first team. The back four of Reid, Clements, McCarthy and Power provided experience, stubborn resistance and a little power. The midfield of David Phillips, Neil McNab and Clive Wilson were all skilful creators but the attack of Lillis, Davies and Simpson was just too powder puff. We were overwhelmed in midfield and did not score enough goals.

Boxing Day brought a rare home victory over Liverpool with a goal from Clive Wilson. It was a bitterly cold day and Liverpool absolutely pounded our goal from first minute to last. Mick McCarthy had one of his best ever games in a City shirt and really put his body on the line by hurling himself in front of everything that Liverpool could offer. Young keeper Eric Nixon threatened to make a name for himself with a brilliant display between the posts. My toes were numb as we left the Kippax in jubilation but no one was really fooled by the result. Yet this result obviously gave the team a real lift and City won five games on the bounce. But for the last of these against Queens Park Rangers there was a crowd of only twenty thousand. The hooliganism, the fences around the grounds, and the general bad press that football got at the time all played their part in this but there is also no denying that the actual football that City were playing was of a poor quality and they did not have any money to do anything about it. We all held our breath as City did not win any of their last thirteen League games of the season.

There was one weekend that stood out amidst the gloom in March 1986 when City played United at Old Trafford on Saturday 22nd in the League followed by a visit to Wembley the next day to play Chelsea in the final of the Full Members Cup which was an unnecessary addition to the fixture calendar. After numerous trips to Old Trafford on public transport in which I took my life in my own hands it was with considerable relief that I accepted a lift in a car from my great pal Phil. We parked down near the cricket ground and my legs turned to jelly as we joined the massed ranks of Reds down by Stretford Town Hall and proceeded to march to the ground. Colours were not as widely worn as today for obvious reasons and I did not spot a single blue as we made our way down Warwick Road past Macari's chippy, behind the Scoreboard End and took up our places alongside the pitch in the paddock in the United Road stand. United were going for the title which they had not won for nearly twenty years. The team managed by Big Ron Atkinson contained Paul McGrath, Norman Whiteside, Gordon Strachan and Mark Hughes. Phil was struggling to see the pitch so tightly were we crammed in as we stood on level with the edge of the penalty area down at the Stretford End. For some unknown reason City wore blue shorts which did not quite match the colour of their shirts. Mick McCarthy missed the game leading to a third first team appearance from Youth team skipper Steve Redmond, he of thunder thighs, great skill and massive heart! "Super" Gordon Davies was also missing with his place taken by Steve Kinsey.

Like many teams before or since at Old Trafford City seemed to freeze as United took the lead through Gibson in the second minute. Phil and I sensed the worst as a tame penalty was converted by Strachan on the hour. The game seemed over and United stopped attacking giving City plenty of possession. Incredibly Clive Wilson nipped in to pull a goal back as Phil and I did our level best not to cheer out loud. We were really put to the test when sensationally Albiston turned it back to the diminutive Turner only to find that he was not there! Two-two! The Reds were stunned. Phil and I could hardly contain ourselves as we shook our heads in mock disappointment. We floated back to the car in a euphoric, albeit silent, state and sped back to Middleton to celebrate!

I did not overdo it as I had to be up early for an eight o'clock start down to London for the Full Members Cup final against Chelsea. I guess this was a kind of Johnstone's Paint Trophy for First Division teams but it was a Wembley cup final after all! Cardinal Langley old boy Pete "Titch" McLaughlin offered to drive Phil and I down to the "Smoke" where we had arranged to meet John Joyce in the pub that he managed near Stamford Bridge. As we entered the pub shortly after midday we soon realised just how close it was to Chelsea's HQ. I mean you could see the ground through the window and the whole place was crammed full to the rafters with Chelsea fans who were a fearsome prospect at any time of the day. I think the fact that we were mates of John the landlord enabled us to survive on this occasion. We were the only "Mancs" on the Tube and when we hit Wembley Way it seemed that we were the only Sky Blues attending the match! Everybody had predicted a record low attendance but as we approached the City end it was clear that many City fans had made the journey South. It was said that the City following numbered thirty thousand and the total attendance was given as 68000 with very few neutrals in the ground. I must admit that the whole occasion felt a little bit strange. It may have been because we played the previous day or perhaps it was due to the media reminding everybody that it was not a "proper" cup final.

There was no such thing as squad rotation so both teams put out full strength sides on consecutive days. Chelsea were without the injured Kerry Dixon but included Pat Nevin, Nigel Spackman and David Speedie in their ranks. City played the same team as at Old Trafford the day before apart from the return of Mick McCarthy for the unlucky Kenny Clements who had picked up an injury. We were in the top tier at the tunnel end where I had stood in '74, '76, and '81. It was great to see Paul Power leading out the team in their classic red and black striped shirts and black shorts. I hoped this was a good omen as I thought of that Neil Young winner in 1969 which I had watched on a friend's colour television as I was not deemed old enough then to travel to London. Within minutes City took the lead as Steve Kinsey scuffed one into the bottom corner at the far end. He never seemed to strike a ball cleanly! Then events became slightly surreal as Chelsea threw everything at City. I do not remember us getting over the half way line as Chelsea cut through our defence with ease. I reassured Phil that it was not a "proper" Cup final as Chelsea scored five goals in the next hour with Speedie grabbing three. With ten minutes left the City end started to empty a la Gillingham '99. Paul Simpson came on as substitute and began to run down the left wing unopposed and put over three or four really good crosses. City fanatic Lillis got his head on to two of them and pulled the score back to a creditable 5-3. But incredibly with seconds left on the watch we were awarded a penalty right in front of us. Lillis tucked it away and there was just chance for one last attack. But it was not to be. I cannot remember any game at the top level ending in a five–all draw let alone a Wembley final! As we left the ground I did not really know what to think. For eighty minutes we had been absolutely hammered yet we had only lost by five goals to four.

City had enough points to survive as the season petered out. The entertainment value was really low and the back page of the Manchester Evening News began to concentrate on the talent that was beginning to emerge in the Youth team which had got to the semi-final of the Youth Cup against Arsenal. A particular article caught my eye about goal machine Paul Moulden who had incredibly scored two hundred and eighty nine goals in a season as a schoolboy for Bolton Lads Club! I entered the main stand for the Arsenal tie shortly after kick off but having no programme and not knowing what the players actually looked like my attention was soon drawn to the tall slim striker with the film star looks. His touch on the ball was so good as he held the ball up and brought others into the game like the tall speedy right winger. I heard one or two shouts of "Go on, Paul" so naturally assumed that this was the great "goalden" Moulden. It was of course Paul Lake. He was head and shoulders the best player on the pitch. I realised that Moulden was in fact the nippy inside forward who was no slouch himself. But he was not in the same league as Paul Lake. This was the youth team which also included Steve Redmond, Andy Hinchcliffe, David White and Ian Brightwell all of whom would go on to play hundreds of times for the first team over the next few years. Significantly City beat Arsenal that night to reach the final but it is a sobering thought that the basis of this Arsenal side including the likes of Michael Thomas and Paul Merson would go onto win the First Division within three years and would enjoy twenty years of success under George Graham and Arsene Wenger. Whereas City...... In the short term, though, this City youth side went on to defeat United in the final before a great crowd of over eighteen thousand including Phil and myself. When Steve Redmond climbed the steps of the main stand to lift the trophy the roof nearly came off the Kippax.

A few weeks later I received a phone call to tell me that my beloved grandad James had been taken ill and was in North Manchester General. It was James who had introduced me to the Blues when I was eight years old back in 1966. He had followed City all his life and attended matches since arriving in England from Ireland in 1923. He had great charisma and I absolutely loved being in his company. Whenever he met somebody on the street the conversation would turn to City. James did not mind calling City himself but he certainly did not like anybody else doing so. It filled me with a heavy heart as I sat by his bedside on Grand National Day. He was charming the nurses with his knowledge of racing and trying to get one of them to place a bet for him. We chatted about City until it was time to go and I was devastated to learn of his death a few days later. I adored my grandad James.

Macker did not attend many games during the 1985-1986 season as he had left Manchester to train to be a priest at Ushaw Training College in County Durham. Although we were all a little surprised, to say the least, Macker explained that he really enjoyed the lifestyle at college. Lectures took place in the mornings but the rest of the day was his. He took to running around the Durham countryside and was becoming a quite accomplished marathon runner. He said that the food was good at the college and he rounded off the day with a few beers in the local pubs. Strangely, he did not really mention religion! He consequently invited a few of us up to the North East for a night out. The centre of Newcastle around the Bigg Market was a real eye opener. While we were wearing jumpers, scarves and coats on a bitterly cold January night the locals were clad in tee shirts and were certainly made of sterner stuff than us. A couple of nights later a Tuesday tea time session in a Sunderland pub was as bleak as it gets. Two old blokes in the corner and a barmaid on roller skates! Indeed as we drove through the area it was clear that the Miner's strike had had a devastating effect with whole villages empty and silent. A rare exception being a wonderful evening in a local miner's club with the piano in the corner pumping out anthems such as "The Blaydon Races" and "Down by the Riverside" to rapturous applause. I felt quite humble sitting quietly in the corner just watching and listening to these men in their fifties and sixties with coal blackened faces from a lifetime down the pit singing their hearts out as they downed pint after pint of Brown Ale. They had already been consigned to the history books by Margaret Thatcher, and what we were witnessing seemed like a defiant last stand. The men seemed so proud. I had tears in my eyes.

Meanwhile City were about to start the new season. The club had no money and badly needed reinforcements on the pitch. Paul Power who had served the club with real distinction and made over four hundred appearances for the club left to join Everton. He would end the season with a well-deserved Championship medal. I was so pleased for him. Although not blessed with the ability of some of his teammates in the great City sides of the late seventies he always gave one hundred per cent. Keeper Alex Williams was struggling to recover from injury so Perry Suckling was signed from Coventry. He was joined by the overweight Trevor Christie from Derby with the popular Lillis going in the other direction! What on earth prompted this transfer? Trevor Christie? They may as well have signed Tony Christie! I think that Trevor Christie and Gordon Davies probably represented the worst pair of strikers that we have ever had. The only solace for true Blues was in the selection of Steve Redmond and Ian Brightwell from the youth team. The Blues won only one of the first seven games before manager Billy McNeill left to join Aston Villa. The penny pinching Blues had no option but to appoint his assistant Jimmy Frizzell who had had great success in the lower divisions with Oldham Athletic as the club continued to remind us.

Frizzell did what most fans would have done. He immediately got rid of "Tony" Christie, signed the experienced Imre Varadi, John Gidman and Tony Grealish, and promoted David White and Paul Moulden from the youth team. On the 4th of November I sat in the main stand amongst a crowd of only four thousand nine hundred to see City defeat Wimbledon in the Full Members Cup with two goals from Paul Moulden. This was the smallest crowd I have ever been part of for a first team game at Maine Road. Moulden repeated this scoring feat a few days later as Villa were defeated in the League but by December 13th City were bottom of the First Division for the visit of West Ham United.

It was absolutely chucking it down as Macker joined me in the centre of the Kippax in our usual place down near the front. It was great to see Macker at the match again and yes he did have his half time tangerine in his pocket. But these were different times. The fence at the front of the stand was now huge. Previously it had resembled a garden gate. And there was so much room on the Kippax that had been jam packed a decade earlier. There were only nineteen thousand in the ground with very few Hammers in the Platt Lane to our left. West Ham were always such an attractive side to watch and were going well at fifth in the Division. Their side contained Phil Parkes in goals, with Tony Gale and Alvin Martin at the back, the stylish Alan Devonshire alongside the combative Paul Ince and Mark Ward in midfield, with dynamic duo Tony Cottee and Frank McAvennie up front. City put out a very experienced side with Suckling in goals, a back four of Gidman, Clements, McCarthy and Wilson, a midfield of Grealish and McNab, David White and Paul Simpson on the wings with Varadi and Moulden up front. Jimmy Frizzell's programme notes reminded us all that City were "playing well and getting nothing". He claimed that "mistakes are killing us week after week". He even questioned about whether City should adopt a more defensive style away from home? Well, with three draws and six defeats from nine games surely this should have told him something. Elsewhere the programme told us that we were in Greenall Whitley land, that the "Today" was the paper for football, and that the top scorers in the First Division included Gary Birtles, Ian Rush, Lee Chapman, Cyrille Regis, Clive Allen and John

Aldridge. The top division contained Wimbledon, Watford, Luton Town, Oxford United and Sheffield Wednesday! Yet we were bottom!

West Ham could not live with a rampant City that day. In a magnificent display of attacking soccer totally out of keeping with recent form City hit three fine goals with two from Varadi and one from David White. West Ham's solitary goal came from the stylish Alan Devonshire. In truth it was like a school match with end to end football on a greasy pitch. Both sides left the field to great applause from both sets of fans who knew that they had witnessed something special. Paul Ince left the field with a real scowl on his face. Some things never change. Two weeks later City were hammered 5-0 at Charlton Athletic!

Imre Varadi and Paul Moulden were linking up well. Although lightweight, Varadi still had great pace and Moulden would "fend off" defenders who were over twice his size before putting the ball in the back of the net. But after a narrow victory on January 3rd against Oxford thanks to a rare Neil McNab strike the wheels came off for City. There were injuries to both wingers White and Simpson but significantly to Moulden which would keep him out for weeks. Old favourite Peter Barnes arrived from United but having been away for eight years seemed a shadow of his former self despite the Kippax willing him to succeed. Kenny Clements and Mick McCarthy were performing heroics at the back every week but the team could not score. The Blues scored only three goals in the next ten matches and when that winless run extended to fourteen matches the unthinkable happened. City were relegated for the second time in four years. Burly striker Paul Stewart was signed from Blackpool at the end of March but it was too little, too late. For the first time in my life I was so disappointed with the way that some of the players seemed to readily accept their fate that I did not attend the last two home games as we were already relegated. Imre Varadi top scored with nine followed by Moulden with a mere five showing where our problems lay.

As City yo-yoed between divisions from 1983 to 1987 I lived in a number of flats and houses in the unfamiliar Prestwich and Whitefield areas of Manchester. I was absolutely delighted when I was tipped off that there was a teaching job coming up at my old school Cardinal Langley in Middleton. Although it was no longer a Grammar school it was one of the greatest feelings in my life to walk through the doors as a teacher at the start of the new term. I felt as though I had served my apprenticeship in such a tough school in Bolton and that I had come home. A few months later I literally had, as I bought a flat near the Old Boar's Head in Middleton. I looked around the staff room with a mixture of delight and trepidation. Although I had left the school as a pupil some nine years earlier there were quite a few senior staff who were still there and I really struggled to call them by their first names. As everyone knows, your teachers remain "Sir" or "Miss" for life. I was totally in awe of my old History master John Durcan, and my ex-French teacher Seamus Crawford. They were absolute idols who I had placed on a pedestal long ago and it seemed unthinkable that I was now a colleague of theirs. Stalwart John McCarron delighted in telling me after every lesson about his relationship with the pupils:

"I hate them and they hate me". Hardly an inspiration to an idealist like myself! I hooked up with Mike Coffey and his fellow teachers from St. Dominics who had recently amalgamated with Cardinal Langley in one of several school reorganisations in the nineteen eighties. A few weeks later a new face appeared in the R.E. department. It was Macker, who had decided that the life of a priest was not for him. I could not have been happier to see him.

Although some of the classes were tough the staff were incredibly supportive. Experienced hands like Brian Kenny and Pete Briggs gave me some invaluable tips on how to handle the "little terrors" and Ray Ashton helped me with organising school football and cricket fixtures. As crowds dropped at Maine Road City began to encourage links with local schools and I started to take small groups of pupils to home matches. We would arrive early and I would pick up the tickets from the ticket office which were usually for the North Stand. One of the many recent security measures at games had been the introduction of a total ban on alcohol on the terraces. Imagine my horror when I spotted one of my eleven year old charges supping a pint of bitter in his seat behind the goal at half time just as the teams came back on the field!

Life at Cardinal Langley was never dull and the second year football team were certainly no slouches. They beat off every challenge as they reached the Catholic Cup Final that year. They contained in their ranks boys like the commanding centre half Dean Kirby, the tiny Paul O'Keefe, and the diminutive ginger haired midfield general Paul Scholes. It was no surprise to see Brian Kidd on the touchline down at St. Bede's as we demolished the opposition to lift the trophy. He had recently been appointed by Alex Ferguson to sort out the youth set up at United and it was not long before the boys were invited down to Old Trafford.

In summer Scholes excelled on the cricket field too. He was a magnificent batsman with a fine array of strokes and tremendous power for a lad of his size. In one particular innings he hit 83 not out against North Manchester High School in little over ten overs. I took great delight in coaching the second year cricket team after school and they proceeded to thrash every side they came up against on their way to winning the Catholic Cup at Xaverian College. They say that pride comes before a fall and I foolishly decided that the boys were now capable of moving up a gear and arranged a friendly with Hulme

Grammar School of Oldham, a school with a proud cricketing tradition. I guess it was the equivalent of winning the Premier League and progressing to the Champions League. On a balmy summer's evening Hulme won the toss and decided to bat first. The majority of their team were on Lancashire's books and were resplendent in their cream flannels and jumpers. One or two of our boys wore black tracksuit trousers and trainers. Our bowling was immediately put to the sword as Hulme amassed a total of 145 runs for three wickets off only 20 overs. Our boys were absolutely crestfallen and clearly intimidated by the surroundings. Hulme Grammar School had its own scoreboard and spectators were sat in deckchairs around the boundary edge. It was all I could do to encourage the boys that all was not lost and that at least we had our pride to play for. I took up my place as Umpire at the bowlers end as the opening bowler handed me his cap and sweater before marking out his run up. He disappeared into the distance. I heard the pounding of his feet and a faint burst of wind as he passed me on the way to the crease. He delivered the ball and it flew into the gloves of the wicket keeper before our batsman could move. The batsman gave me a rueful look as the bowler took a piece of paper from his pocket and marked a dot ball on it. The next ball our batsman moved his bat a little, the ball caught the edge and the keeper claimed the catch. 0 for 1. I feared the worst, but was relieved as we scraped into double figures. Unfortunately 11 for 1 soon became 11 for 7 and we were finally all out for 19. We had lost by 126 runs. I often wonder whether Paul Scholes ever recalled such an evening as he proceeded to pick up Premiership title after title and medal after medal in his wonderful career with Manchester United and England?

Are you watching Brian Kidd? Refereeing at Cardinal Langley in 1987.

NINE.

STRANGE FRUIT.

City were again back in the Second Division with new club sponsors Brother and yet another new manager, Mel Machin from Norwich City. Mick McCarthy left to sign for Celtic after four excellent years with the club and local boy Clive Wilson was snapped up by Chelsea. Yet I felt incredibly optimistic about the new season. I felt that this was to be the year that the youngsters from the all-conquering youth team would really come to the fore. On the opening day of the season against Plymouth Argyle the slight but skilful Ian Scott and the tenacious full back Andy Hinchcliffe joined Steve Redmond, David White and Ian Brightwell in the first team. Paul Lake, who was the best of the lot, could not even make the substitute's bench which for the first time included an extra thirteenth player. I think Lake suffered initially due to the fact that he could play almost anywhere in the side! A little bit like Paul Madeley of the great Leeds side of the Seventies who was invariably substitute as he could replace practically anybody in the side without the team losing any of its effectiveness.

After a narrow victory over Plymouth Macker, Phil and I caught the bus up to Oldham a week later for the Boundary Park fixture. The calendar told us that it was August but I have never seen such rain like that on the open Rochdale Road End that afternoon. There was simply no hiding place from the elements. Imre Varadi nipped in to score City's goal at the Chadderton End in a one all draw and we set off to walk home before arriving in Middleton like drowned rats. Foolishly I was wearing some trendy summer moccasins but these had to be consigned to the dustbin as they were completely ruined. My "Nick Heyward style" fair-isle jumper now stretched just below my knees and met a similar fate. I think I spotted one or two inflatable bananas on the terraces that day, too. A paddling pool would have been more appropriate but they came a little later.

September brought the devastating news that my favourite band The Smiths had broken up. Their final album "Strangeways, Here We Come" and subsequent South Bank Show served as a fitting epitaph. Meanwhile the Blues had to scrap for every point as they tried to acclimatise to life in a new division. Yet when they did hit their stride they were unstoppable. Stewart and Varadi were banging in goals for fun as Millwall, Stoke, and Leicester were hammered in successive home games in September. City had not produced football like this on a regular basis for years. It was worrying though that home gates were as low as only fifteen thousand in midweek and struggling to reach twenty thousand at the weekend. I began to wonder whether the last four years or so had been too much to put up with for too many City fans. Or had football simply gone out of fashion with its years of hooliganism, the Bradford and Heysel tragedies, and general lack of family-friendly facilities?

There was nothing but grey skies over Manchester when I opened my bedroom curtains on Saturday 7th November 1987. The visit of Huddersfield Town to Maine Road held little appeal. A couple of lunch time phone calls confirmed the fact that I would be on my own for this one. What on earth were the Granada T.V. vans doing here I thought as I rounded the corner by the Souvenir shop? Little did I and the other nineteen thousand five hundred and eighty two fans know what the afternoon had in store. This is surely the beauty of football! City put ten goals past Huddersfield with hat tricks from Paul Stewart, David White, and reserve Tony Adcock who had replaced the injured Imre Varadi. Paul Lake was majestic and both David White and Paul Simpson had arguably their best games for the club. Huddersfield wore dreadful yellow checked shirts, were managed by the bullish Malcolm McDonald and when years later their full back Malcolm

Brown turned up at a school parents evening I could not look him in the eye. Huddersfield's goal in the 10-1 mauling was even scored by ex- Blue Andy May from the penalty spot. The afternoon did not get light and the rain did not stop but it was as perfect a day as you could get. Instead of going out and getting plastered I decided to take a leaf out of Bob Paisley's book. When he was once asked how he celebrated Liverpool's European Cup triumph in 1977 he famously replied "With a cup of tea. I wanted to remember every minute of it". On that November evening in 1987 I contacted my brother Pete who I had not seen in a while and we drove up onto the moors above Oldham for a quiet pint in a half empty pub. I replayed every goal over and over to the dismay of a clearly bored brother Pete.

Hopes were high as City went into the New Year but points were frittered away and it became clear that our best chance of success lay in the F.A. Cup. It took three games to get past Huddersfield, two to get past Blackpool and one to defeat Plymouth Argyle. The Blues were drawn against the mighty Liverpool in a televised Sixth Round tie on a Sunday at Maine Road. As the teams took to the pitch in the spring sunshine it was clear to me that the scene was set for a huge mis-match. City's promising youngsters lined up against giants such as John Barnes, Peter Beardsley, Craig Johnston, Bruce Grobbelaar , Alan Hansen and Mark Lawrenson. I felt isolated on the steps of a packed Kippax as all those around me roared on their favourites in the first frantic minutes of the match. It was true that we were giving as good as we got as the tackles flew in. But I saw in the faces of the Liverpool players just what we were lacking. Experience and know-how. When they got the ball they kept it. They stroked the ball around the back four and through the midfield effortlessly as they waited for one of our defenders to be pulled out of position. Eventually after half an hour Barnes was released down the left wing before he pulled the ball back for Republic of Ireland international Ray Houghton to drive the ball home. I realised that they were controlling the game and that although this City side were full of attacking endeavour and gut bursting effort we were still an awful long way from the top of the game. Liverpool hit three further goals in the second half which flattered them and the papers and media pundits praised the efforts of the valiant Blues. But this did not hide the fact that City were now a selling club. Weeks later Graeme Souness was photographed in disguise on a scouting mission in the North Stand, and it was no surprise when star striker Paul Stewart was sold to Spurs in April.

If I was in any doubt about the standing of City as the 1988-1989 season opened then one glance at the team sheet confirmed my worst suspicions. The Blues had received £1.7 million for Stewart and bought players who would not have got into the reserves a few years earlier. At the beginning of the decade my heroes were Joe Corrigan, Dennis Tueart, Asa Hartford, Tommy Hutchison and for a season at least Trevor Francis. The side which entertained Oldham Athletic at the end of August 1988 contained the likes of Andy Dibble, Brian Gayle, Wayne Biggins and Trevor Morley, with Nigel Gleghorn and Mark Seagraves in the squad. Neil McNab was still giving everything in midfield but there was just not the quality to support the inexperienced stars of the 1986 youth team who made up the backbone of the side. Steve Redmond was a tower of strength in defence, Andy Hinchcliffe was deadly at free kicks and corners, David White had blistering pace, Ian Brightwell gave every ounce in whatever position he was asked to play, and Paul Lake was just a magnificent footballer. Without these "lads" I doubt that anybody would have turned up to watch Manchester City in the late eighties.

There were only twenty two thousand fans in attendance for this Bank Holiday derby. As I approached the ground it seemed appropriate that the music on my Walkman was Morrissey's "Every Day is like Sunday" in which the singer wails about a seaside town that they had forgotten to close down. Maine Road had become the football ground "that they had forgotten to close down" with its four ill-matched stands, high grey fences, huge gaps on the terraces, and a general lack of fresh paint and care. Missing the company of Phil and Macker who seemed to have given up the ghost I took up a seat in the main stand and hoped for the best. Lakey scored a fine goal but we were totally outplayed in the second half by a Roger Palmer inspired display as the Latics hit back with four goals. Rock bottom after only two games. But then as now the Second Division was a very tight league and the difference quality-wise between top and bottom was very slender. Paul Moulden was recalled to the starting line-up and the Blues put together a run of five victories which hauled us right up the table to fourth. This run included a rare victory over Chelsea at Stamford Bridge before an unbelievably low crowd of only eight thousand!

On Boxing Day the trip to Stoke just about encapsulated everything that was City at that time. I managed to prise Brian Kenny from the staff room to accompany me down to the Victoria Ground in my new Micra. I have always been a reluctant driver and it took me years to realise that the two outside lanes of the motorway were part of the same road as I hugged the inside lane for dear life. When we eventually arrived in the Potteries and parked up it was clear that the City following that day was enormous and later reckoned to be about fifteen thousand out of a total attendance of just over twenty four thousand. The majority were in fancy dress. Vicars and tarts thronged the side streets as Dracula and Frankenstein passed by carrying a huge inflatable paddling pool. There were thousands of bananas of course but I nearly choked on mine as the team took to the field carrying one each. Brian and I were sat with thousands of Blues in the stand opposite the player's entrance and City filled at least two of the four stands. The atmosphere was phenomenal! Manager Mel Machin had again chosen to leave out Paul Moulden for this one so the strike force consisted of Trevor Morley and Wayne Biggins with Nigel

Gleghorn on the left. The Stoke players were still laughing at the crowd when we took the lead through Nigel Gleghorn, who has since become a much better radio pundit than he was a footballer. He made Paul Power seem like Lionel Messi. Anyway, the Blues, unlike their formidable support, tamely folded as Stoke equalised just before half time and went on to win by three goals to one. I think it would be fair to say that the City support that day was awesome. What a shame about the football that the Blues served up. "Swales Out" was beginning to rival "Come On, City" as the favourite chant of the supporters with "You are not fit to wear the shirt" coming much later although it could have applied to half of this team.

City began to hit something which resembled consistency with strong home victories over Hull, Ipswich and Leicester. The latter game on March the 11th though was memorable for all the wrong reasons as local hero Paul Lake spent an agonising twenty minutes on the deck after swallowing his tongue after a collision with a defender. The ground became eerily silent as each minute ticked by and it is probably no exaggeration to state that trainer Roy Bailey and club doctor Mr. Luft saved the life of Paul Lake that afternoon. Incredibly he returned to the side just a week later.

On the 15th of April with City tucked in in second place behind leaders Chelsea Macker and I made the short journey to Blackburn who themselves were hopeful of a place in the play-offs. The sun was shining brightly as we took up our place behind a huge fence at the Darwen End of the ground. We were disappointed that Lakey was out for this one and his place was to be taken by the statuesque Gerry Taggart. It did seem that City had a penchant for playing centre halves at full back, but against a tricky winger it was like playing against dustbins. Straight from the kick off Taggart was cruelly exposed as crosses were pulled back from the touchline with alarming regularity and shots rained in on the City goal. Up front David White was running into blind alleys and the strike force of Jason Donovan look-a-like David Oldfield and Trevor Morley were completely ineffective. Blackburn hit four goals without reply and it was a really poor performance from a City side who before this match had seemed to be heading for Division One. Our grumbles and groans were soon put into perspective. We got back to the car just in time for the trademark theme tune of Sports Report on Radio Two at five o'clock. We were rooted to the spot as reports came through from Hillsborough telling of the dreadful events of the day as ninety six Liverpool fans lost their lives at the Cup semi-final. As we looked around it was clear that supporters in their cars were similarly stunned upon hearing the news. There was a real hush all around broken only by crackling voices coming from car radios along the street. Only minutes earlier we had been castigating Mel Machin for his team selection and David White for his poor crossing. How ridiculous this all seemed. Nobody spoke on the return journey. News reports came in throughout the evening. My brother Paul upon hearing the news had caught a train over to Merseyside to be with his girlfriend. The scenes he described on Lime Street Station were lamentable as fans were being met by loved ones upon their return from Sheffield. The quiet dignity of all on the station being in huge contrast to the disgraceful picture created by the Sun newspaper of the behaviour of Liverpool supporters on that tragic afternoon.

Thoughts eventually returned to football and on Monday the first of May high-flying Crystal Palace were the visitors for a top of the table clash at Maine Road. Resplendent in their fantastic red and blue striped shirts they contained the likes of Ian Wright and Mark Bright in their ranks and were sure to provide a real test for the young City side who were boosted by the return of both Paul Moulden and Paul Lake. The crowd of 33000 was twelve thousand up on the previous home game and the sun was uncharacteristically beating down as the teams took to the field. City's young back four of Lake, Brightwell, Redmond and Hinchcliffe were solid while the experienced Megson and McNab controlled the midfield. But it was David White who took the eye. It was one of those days when everything clicked and he really flew down the wing leaving defenders in his wake and what is more he was providing a stream of pinpoint crosses into the box. It was from one of these that Nigel Gleghorn arrived at the far post to put City into a well-deserved lead in front of the Palace fans at the Platt Lane End. The only downer on a brilliant first half performance was the fact that keeper Andy Dibble seemed to be injured and was unable to take any dead ball kicks. The team left the field to a great reception and with only two games remaining the First Division was almost within reach. But this was City and it was never going to be that simple. Andy Dibble was indeed injured and unable to resume his position for the second half. There were only two substitutes in 1989 and it would have been most unusual for one of these to have been a goalkeeper. The green jersey was worn by Nigel Gleghorn who claimed to have been an excellent cricketer in his youth! This was a huge test and right from the kick off Palace sensed that City were here for the taking. I am sure that the visitors sensed the complete feeling of unease that has enveloped Maine Road so many times over the years. City were much more cautious in their approach and seemed hell bent on preserving their lead. The fans cheered every time Gleghorn made even the simplest of catches and roared with elation as he dived to push a shot round the post. The great Ian Wright equalised with a piledriver after 75 minutes but hero Gleghorn and City held firm for a priceless point. Two games to go!

The following Saturday Bournemouth provided the opposition for what was supposed to be a stroll back into the big time. They were led by Harry Redknapp who was just taking his first steps in what would be a great managerial career and contained the experienced Kevin Bond, Shaun Teale and Luther Blissett in their squad. Blissett previously played for Watford and was sensationally signed by world famous AC Milan. It is widely rumoured that they slipped up in their scouting network that day and that they meant to sign Watford's other coloured player, the great John Barnes. It did not take them long to realise their mistake with Blissett returning within a year for a knockdown price. Unforturately by then Barnes had been snapped up by Liverpool and went on to have a great career at Anfield.

There was a great feeling of celebration in the air as two goals from Paul Moulden and another from Trevor Morley gave the Blues an unassailable three goal lead at half time. Chickens were counted in the stands, maps to Anfield, Highbury and Old Trafford were dusted down and incredibly Paul Lake revealed years later that down in the dressing rooms comedian Eddie Large was delivering a half time team talk! This could only happen at Manchester City. How unprofessional can you get? There is just no way that this should have been allowed to happen! I never could understand why a comedian was allowed to sit on the bench for first team games. Was he a "better" fan than anybody else? How do you measure the support of an individual? Or love of your club?

What happened next was pure City. The teams emerged into the sunshine with a carnival taking place on the terraces. The Blues were clearly thinking of their summer holidays as passes began to go astray. McNab and Megson were suddenly second to the ball as young Scouser Ian Bishop began to stroke the ball across the turf with pinpoint accuracy. Bournemouth pulled a goal back. Mere consolation. Then another. Surely not? The game went into the ninetieth minute. With fingernails once again bitten to the quick over thirty thousand fans implored the referee to blow the whistle. This he did, but he was pointing to the penalty spot. A penalty to Bournemouth in the last minute of added time! What a nightmare. The much maligned Blissett stepped forward to beat Cooper and give Bournemouth a share of the points. I do not think that I have ever been so annoyed leaving Maine Road as I was that afternoon. It is a good job that I knew nothing of events down in the dressing room at half time.

As the final Saturday of the season dawned the task facing City was simple. They needed a draw from the visit to Bradford to ensure promotion back to the top flight. Only four years after the Bradford fire tickets were very hard to come by for this one and it was almost a relief when my final attempt ended in failure. Instead I decided to get the number 17 bus into Manchester to buy the new Stone Roses LP that everybody was raving about. It turned out to be the last vinyl album that I ever bought. I had taken to buying cassettes which I could also play on the car radio or on my Walkman, but you cannot beat the thrill of opening an album gatefold on the bus home and taking in the fantastic artwork while examining the track list of the yet unknown songs. A lyric sheet was the icing on the cake! The Stone Roses took my breath away as I anxiously eyed the clock as kick off approached. I was like a cat on a hot tin roof as I alternated between the Roses and the City commentary on good old GMR. I just could not let the commentary flow for fear that Bradford would score. Half way through the first half they duly took the lead and as the clock ticked inevitably towards half past four the Blues were still one down and seemingly doomed to another desperate year in division Two. And then it happened….Moulden passed the ball to White who strangely was on the left wing. He centred and there was Trevor Morley to prod the ball home from six yards out. The Blues had done it! I danced around my living room as time seemed to stand still. A solitary celebration in a Middleton flat that meant so much. Moments that mattered far more than the interminable hours carousing around the pubs of Manchester later that night. "There's only one Trevor Morley". Thank goodness for that.

TEN.

FINE TIMES.

As the eighties came to a close the Berlin Wall came down, tanks drove through Tiananmen Square and "Madchester" spawned the Second Summer of Love. The jewel in the crown was a former yacht showroom on Whitworth Street West which was transformed into the world-renowned Hacienda by owners New Order. What on earth was a yacht showroom doing in late eighties Manchester? I could understand it in the newly gentrified era of the twenty first century. But back then? On my single visit to the Hacienda I found that the reality did not match the myth. Perhaps it was a bad night that I had chosen, but as I looked around at the baggy jean clad regulars "grooving" in the sparse interior I felt as if I was at somebody else's party. I was after all pushing thirty! I guess my party was back in the mid-seventies at Pips, Rafters and Cellar V. I felt more comfortable in Corbieres or Mr. Thomas's on Cross Street from where I would move on to the Continental on Harter Street famous for its Nurses' night, tacky mural, Greek owners and dubious donner kebabs!

There were great gigs to catch away from the mainstream Apollo and Free Trade Hall. I managed to see Joe Strummer and his Mescaleros at the International and John Cooper Clarke with backing band at the Gallery. I was surprised to find myself stood alongside the Happy Mondays at the International one night taking in Sixties folk hero Donovan. The pub scene was changing in Manchester and all of a sudden it was cool to be of Irish descent. Van Morrison was on the juke box and Irish bars were springing up everywhere. We would go into Mulligans off Deansgate or down to O'Sheas for a pint of the black stuff. The Mancunian equivalent of The Pogues were probably Toss The

Feathers and we would try to see them at the 32 Club in Ardwick Green as often as we could. They may not have had a Shane McGowan but they sure could play.

The biggest indication that City were back in the big time was the signing of Clive Allen, formerly of Spurs but plying his trade in France. He was the first star signing since Trevor Francis and cost the club a million pounds that they probably could not afford. The further signing of Ian Bishop compensated fans for the fact that Paul Moulden moved in the other direction. Despite his popularity with the Blues supporters it may be fair to say that the Second Division was probably his true level. Allen made his debut in an opening day defeat at Anfield, scored the winner over Q.P.R. but was absent injured by the time United came to Maine Road on the 23rd of September.

A bright autumn day saw Macker and I replaying the past ourselves by getting the bus into town and leaving the car at home with the intention of having a few beers after the match. In celebration of course! There was little real hope of this as the Blues must have been the biggest underdogs of all time. What little experience we had in the shape of Clive Allen and Neil McNab was confined to the treatment table as the Blues languished joint bottom of the table with four points from six games. United only had three more points but their team was full of internationals like Viv Anderson, Gary Pallister, Paul Ince, Brian McClair and Mark Hughes. Thankfully skipper Bryan Robson was injured and would sit this one out. I reckoned that our best chance lay in the fact that their Scottish keeper Jim Leighton was really dodgy if any kind of pressure was put upon him. We took up our old position right in the centre of the Kippax just enough steps up from the front to be able to see over the giant perimeter fence. It was reassuring to see so many familiar faces around us including of course Big Ted and the bus drivers. Who drove the buses on a Saturday afternoon? I tried hard not to let on to Macker just how nervous I was about the prospect of an absolute battering from the Reds. As kick off approached there was a particularly tense atmosphere in the stands. In a packed stadium I noted that it was strange that an entire section of the Platt Lane stand where it joined the main stand remained curiously empty. The reason for this was soon to become clear.

A huge roar announced the entry of the two teams. Paul Cooper deputised for Dibble in goals with a back four of Fleming, Gayle, Redmond and Hinchcliffe. Ian Brightwell replaced McNab alongside Ian Bishop and Paul Lake in midfield. David Oldfield partnered Trevor Morley up front with David White on the right wing. The game had hardly settled down before fighting erupted behind the goal at the North Stand. It was clear that huge numbers of United fans had somehow obtained tickets for this end and as the police struggled to restore order the teams actually left the pitch. Even in the darkest days of football hooliganism in the seventies and eighties Maine Road had managed largely to escape the kind of behaviour that so blighted the game. Hundreds of United fans were escorted around the pitch to a crescendo of boos before being placed in the empty section of the Platt Lane stand. The mere fact that this section was used in this way indicated to me that the police must have known about the huge number of United fans with tickets for the "wrong" end of the ground. As the teams were brought back by referee Neil Midgley the nightmare soon turned into absolute dreamland!

City were suddenly quicker to the ball all over the pitch. Steve Redmond powered into tackles, David White flew along the wing, Ian Bishop was picking out colleagues at will, and Paul Lake was dancing through a static United defence. Mark Hughes alone frightened me to death. City took the lead with a David Oldfield miscue, Trevor Morley prodded home a second with Leighton prostrate on the deck, and Ian Bishop slotted in a diving header as the Blues went in at half time with a sensational three goal lead! The noise on the Kippax was incredible. Already to my left streams of United fans were leaving the ground. All thoughts of crowd trouble were blown away by such a magnificent performance from City. My heart was in my mouth for about five minutes as Hughes scored an absolute corker for United but this was our day! Oldfield made it four and then Andy Hinchcliffe scored what must rank as one of the all-time great goals at Maine Road. Ian Bishop picked the ball up in midfield and hit a magnificent ball out to David White on the right wing in the shadow of the Main stand. At this point Hinchcliffe set off from just in front of us in the Kippax to somehow meet White's superb first time cross into the box and plant his header firmly past Leighton into the corner of a bulging net! He turned and cheekily raised his arm in triumph towards the dwindling band of Reds just to remind them of the score. Manchester City 5 Manchester United 1.

A sea of sky blue and white left the Kippax as one and flooded out onto the streets of Moss Side in absolute ecstasy. Two hours later we found ourselves in a City pub deep in the heart of Levenshulme of all places! The beer was flowing, the songs were sung and a splendid time was had by all. I recovered in time to watch the highlights on Sunday afternoon just to make sure that it had not all been just a dream.

This should have been the start of a surge up the table by the Blues but despite beating Luton Town the following week at Maine Road results were hard to come by. On November 11th I nipped out of a tedious wedding reception in South Manchester to buy the Football Pink from a nearby newsagents to see how City had gone on away at struggling Derby County. I could not believe my eyes. We had been beaten six nil! This was the biggest defeat that I had ever known and Peter Swales responded by sacking manager Mel Machin within a fortnight. New manager Howard Kendall arrived with a great pedigree but proceeded to turn City into an Everton Old Boys Club by signing Peter Reid, Alan Harper, Wayne Clarke and Adrian Heath. What is more he upset a lot of people by getting rid of fan's favourite Ian Bishop who along with Trevor Morley were exchanged for West Ham's combative ex-Oldham winger Mark Ward. Howard's first game was live on television at Everton and it must go down as the most boring goalless draw of all time. Both sides were lucky to get nil. There were narrow victories over Norwich and Millwall before the return derby fixture against United at Old Trafford on the 3rd of February.

Tickets were quickly sold out from Maine Road but I noticed in the Manchester Evening News that they were on open sale at Old Trafford so I drove down one night after work and bought two tickets for the Stretford Paddock which ran alongside the pitch. I guess that United simply did not expect City fans to have the audacity to just turn up at Old Trafford. But United, too, were having a poor season and were averaging only 37000 for home matches that season.

Saturday dawned and I had that familiar derby day feeling in my stomach. I even felt ill the previous week when I went down to buy the tickets and the ground was deserted. I could not eat any breakfast and after struggling through a cheese sandwich and Football Focus I heard the familiar toot of the horn from Macker's car. We hardly spoke as we made the unfamiliar journey up past Heaton Park and over past Agecroft Colliery in the general direction of that dark place. We parked down by the cricket ground and joined the hordes marching along Warwick Road, past the numerous stalls selling MUFC "tat" and onto the concourse by the Souvenir Shop. A sea of red and white as far as the eye could see. Police on horseback and stacks of orange clad stewards protected the small queues of Blues outside the Scoreboard End. Not a single City fan sported any colours. I felt sick as we entered the turnstiles, bought a programme and made our way right up to the half way line and took up our place right behind the dug-out. I had stood in this exact position on the day that Denis Law condemned the Reds to the Second Division back in 1974. As the ground filled up it was clear that the paddock consisted of mainly middle aged United fans but there were also many groups of teenagers and twenty somethings not wearing any colours. So I decided not to let my allegiances be known. I had got used to this since following the Blues away in the days before segregation in the mid- seventies. I had never seen so many empty spaces at Old Trafford for a derby yet the Blues' section in the Scoreboard End was as tightly packed as always.

The atmosphere was strangely low key for such an important match and I actually started to enjoy the game especially seeing as City were having so much of the play attacking the Stretford End to our left. Wayne Clarke was having a particularly poor game and although being a dead ringer for his brother Alan, or "Sniffer" as he was known, he had little of his footballing ability. Clarke, Brightwell and White all missed easy chances in the first half and Blackmore gave United the lead against the run of play. My heart sank immediately as I anticipated another defeat, but I realised that huge sections of the crowd around us had not cheered the goal. When Ian Brightwell scored from at least thirty five yards we were right behind him and knew that his blockbuster was goal bound from the minute it left his foot. All around us the crowd went crazy. There were thousands of Blues in the Stretford Paddock and even in the Stretford End. The bloke in front of me turned round and said "How have all this lot got in here?" I just shrugged and grinned sheepishly. I was glad to take a draw and at the end of the game was relieved as always to get back to the car unscathed.

A few weeks later I travelled down to Nottingham where I met up with Dave Lamb and we stood on the open end where we had a great view of Andy Dibble's "finest" moment in a City shirt. City had really tightened up at the back under Kendall thanks mainly to Mel Machin's last signing Colin Hendry who was forming a terrific partnership with Steve Redmond. Peter Reid, although he looked about sixty, was tearing around the midfield like a spring chicken giving great encouragement to Lake and Brightwell in particular. It must have been a huge relief to them to be partnered by such an experienced international after being expected to carry the team on their young shoulders. This City side did not like getting beat and it showed. The game appeared to be heading for a draw when Dibble held the ball on his outstretched palm as he looked around the field. "He is behind you" we should have all shouted in unison, but to no avail little Gary Crosby came from behind Dibble to nod the ball off his hand and tap the ball into an empty net. To everybody's amazement including Crosby's the referee awarded a goal!

City were off the bottom but too many games were ending in draws. For some reason or other Kendall did not favour Clive Allen and it was clear that a striker was needed if we were to climb the table. Thus, in March Kendall signed the great Niall Quinn from Arsenal. He made his debut against Chelsea and immediately made a difference. He gave the whole side a focal point and as his confidence rose game by game then so did City's. The following week there were prisoners on the roof of Strangeways as the Blues went down to Villa for a televised game and inspired by Peter Reid stole all three points.

The relegation clouds lifted and for once City fans could look to enjoy the summer World Cup in Italy and look forward with great confidence to the season ahead. They had finally got the manager they needed and despite his over reliance on Everton old boys he did seem to understand the game and be capable of delivering a side that the City fans deserved. Niall Quinn starred for the Republic of Ireland, Pavarotti sang Nessum Dorma, and we all cried with Paul Gascoigne as England tumbled out heroically at the semi-final stage.

ELEVEN.

THE CHANGING OF THE GUARD.

There was a different feel to the game in 1990 than in previous years. The World Cup had provided a real feel good factor from England's performances to the Cameroon goal celebrations. But the fans were changing too. The game probably could fall no lower after the tragedies of Heysel, Hillsborough and Bradford. The fences, draconian police tactics, I.D. cards and closed circuit television within grounds, though deemed necessary, were not the way forward. It had to come from the fans themselves. The birth of the fanzines like "Blue Print", "King of the Kippax" and "Electric Blue", along with the inflatables and fancy dress all helped bring fun back to the terraces but were not as news worthy as a good punch up. Crucially, it could be argued that many teens and twenties who may have been up for trouble were instead attracted to the new youth culture of dance, drugs and electronic music. In short they were more interested in "taking a trip" than "having a go if they thought they were hard enough". As usual Manchester was at the forefront as Acid House dancers "tranced out" and "loved up" at raves in the old warehouses of the industrial wasteland.

The new season opened and I was pleased to see the Blues sign highly rated goalkeeper Tony Coton but dismayed along with thousands of others as Andy Hinchcliffe was exchanged for Neil Pointon who was not really in the same league. But he did play for Everton. I thought his nickname of "Dissa" summed up the deal with Hinchcliffe later going on to play for England. The City side that opened the season against the Gazza-inspired Spurs had a back four of Brightwell, Hendry, Lake and Pointon with former skipper Steve Redmond on the bench. Sensationally Paul Lake was appointed captain and in interviews Kendall talked about building his side around the highly rated Lakey.

The midfield consisted of Harper, Reid, White and Ward with little Adrian Heath alongside Quinny up front. Disappointingly the Blues opened with a defeat, and the home victory over Aston Villa was marred by what looked like a serious injury to Paul Lake. By the time Macker and I travelled to Sunderland on the 3rd of November the Blues were in fifth place and unbeaten since the opening day. As in many previous seasons there was still a huge discrepancy beaten home and away form. At home City had four wins and a draw, but away it was four draws and a defeat.

It was my first visit to Roker Park. The first sign that things were changing on the terraces was the fact that Macker and I were able to go into the pub right outside the away end where fans mixed really well in their team colours. I was amazed by this, having spent the last fifteen or sixteen years attending away matches incognito. At first I stood in the corner by the jukebox just waiting for it to "go off". We chatted to two or three Sunderland lads who actually invited us to stand with them on their end behind the goal. New Order's Balearic beats from their brilliant album "Technique" were greeted with a cheer as we downed pints of the ropey local Vaux beer. It seemed almost a shame to leave the pub. We had struck up such great rapport that we decided to join these friendly Black Cats. We walked behind the City end which was open to the elements and joined the queue for the home terrace! Roker Park was captured in a total time warp. The Taylor Report recommendations of all seater stadiums and all ticket matches had not yet been implemented. There were terraces behind both goals and a paddock in front of the seats. The rain started to fall in true Mancunian style as I devoured the match programme and consumed a tongue numbing Bovril from a cardboard cup. A nationwide round up told me that leading goalscorers included Beardsley, Barnes and Rush from Liverpool, Limpar and Merson from Arsenal, Gascoigne and Lineker from Spurs and Davenport and Gabbiadini from Sunderland. A superb four page spread on City reflected on the three all draw with United a week earlier when Peter Reid left the pitch with only 10 minutes to go with City leading by three goals to one. Unfortunately a slip by sub Ian Brightwell brought the Reds a second which became three and almost four in the dying seconds. The article concluded with the belief that City had the potential to challenge for major honours!

The Sunderland side contained many journeymen like Kevin Ball, Gary Bennett, Gordon Armstrong, and Peter Davenport. We should have been too good for them but had to be content with yet another away draw. David White scored for City with ex-Red Davenport replying for Sunderland. While the game itself was unremarkable it had been a really enjoyable day and we kept in contact with the Sunderland lads in the hope of returning the compliment later in the season. We rounded off the day in Newcastle's Bigg Market before boarding the last train back to Manchester. Incredibly our balloon was to burst on Monday morning when it was announced that Howard Kendall had left to rejoin Everton! Here we go again.

I have always had a special feeling about the fixture City versus Tottenham Hotspur at Maine Road. This is probably due to the fact that this was the first game I saw in October 1966 with my dad. Pat Jennings and Jimmy Greaves were my childhood heroes along with Lee, Bell and Summerbee of course. Who could forget the famous "Ballet On Ice" in the championship winning season? City's demolition of Spurs on a snow covered pitch with that orange ball remains indelibly printed on my memory. It was certainly my favourite match until the 1989 five-one Maine Road massacre. When Spurs came to town on December 15th they were riding high in third place in the First Division. There was no Jennings and Greaves but their side did contain Gary Lineker, Paul Gascoigne, Paul Stewart, Nayim and Pat Van Den Hauwe who was another ex- Everton full back! City, who were now managed by Peter Reid, had got a rare point at Anfield and were just outside the top four. If they could turn some of their draws into wins then they had a real chance of qualifying for Europe. Steve Redmond had regained his place alongside Colin Hendry in the back four and Gary Megson had re-established himself in midfield alongside Reid and Mark Ward. David White had managed to hit a real vein of form feeding off the many flicks and nod downs from the Mighty Quinn. "Quinny" was the new darling of Maine Road. This was not just because he was a really good player who scored goals. It was also because everybody could see that he gave everything that he had in the City cause. This is what City fans love the most. Somebody who is taking their place on the field. Doing what they would do! Quinny did not have to kiss his badge. You just knew.

Maine Road was not covered in snow but it was shrouded in mist and the drizzle was omnipresent as the teams took to the field, with Spurs in all yellow. There was only one team change for City with the return of Tony Coton in goal. As I crossed out Dibble's name on the back of my programme I noticed the colour picture of the new stand at Bradford beneath the teamsheets. Spurs opened brightly with lots of slick passing and a familiar feeling returned to my stomach. They were running rings around us and when star man Gascoigne rounded off a five man move to give them the lead I feared the worst. Coton saved at the foot of the post from Lineker who was through on goal and City did well to reach half time only a goal down. I was dismayed by the mutterings and grumblings of the middle aged supporters in the bar at half time. It was a fantastic game! I have never understood the pessimistic nature of City fans even though I shared it myself. I would never boo my own team or crucify one of our players. Indeed Adrian Heath was suffering from the same abuse meted out to Ian Bowyer before him and Richard Edghill afterwards. The second half performance from City rammed the boos and catcalls back down the throats of the so-called fans. We battered Spurs right from the kick off but left it very late to actually win the match. Fifteen minutes from time Ward equalised from the penalty spot and we laid siege to the Spurs goal down at the North Stand. Redmond hit the bar. It just would not go in. But from the rebound substitute Wayne Clarke rifled the ball in. Maine Road absolutely erupted! We had done it!

It was clear that Peter Reid had steadied the ship and the Blues were in sixth position in the table when Derby County provided the opposition on 20th April 1991 for what was to be one of the most memorable games ever played at Maine Road. Derby were managed by the dour Arthur Cox and were on the verge of certain relegation from Division One. They relied heavily on the veteran Peter Shilton in goal and Mark Wright in defence. Up front they had a good partnership between Mick Harford and the speedy Dean Saunders. Unfortunately the rest of the team were simply triers and runners. They were no match for a City team who were really flying. After half an hour City were two up and cruising with goals from Niall Quinn and David White. I was even starting to think in terms of the Huddersfield game as my mind wandered. It was that easy. Then Derby mounted an attack. The ball was slipped through to Saunders down at the Platt Lane End, City dozed off, and he was through on goal. Coton rushed off his line and as Saunders attempted to go round him he brought him down. Penalty! The referee brandished a red card and Coton was off! Everything had seemed so simple. But things are never that straightforward at City. I was a little disappointed when I saw Niall Quinn pulling on the green jersey. I would have preferred it if maybe Steve Redmond or new signing Andy Hill would have donned the shirt. The words had hardly left my mouth when Niall dived to his left to produce a fingertip save from Saunders' well struck penalty kick. The cheers were as loud as any goal celebrations. Niall left his line to collect the resultant corner to huge roars from the Kippax. There was an absolute carnival atmosphere inside Maine Road. Niall Quinn was the hero of the hour. He could do no wrong in the eyes of his adoring fans. Derby pulled a late goal back but Quinn and the City team were cheered to the rafters as they left the field that day.

City hit five at Villa with David White grabbing four before bringing the season to a close with the visit of Sunderland, who like Derby were on the verge of relegation. Only a win would give them a chance of staying up. I have rarely witnessed such a fantastic away following as that which Sunderland brought to Maine Road that day. There were Red and White stripes everywhere outside the stadium and the Platt Lane was absolutely packed out. The roars that met the two teams were worthy of any cup final and the match too did not disappoint. It was end to end Roy of the Rovers stuff even though there was nothing riding on it for us. David White again starred as City edged a five goal thriller. We had managed to arrange to meet our mates from Sunderland before the game but we were a little bit apprehensive about how they would react to their relegation. I need not have worried. Still bedecked in Red and White they joined myself, Macker and Geordie Steve Price in posh eaterie The Grinch off Cross Street and shrugged off their defeat with a few beers and many laughs late into the evening. A great night rounded off a great season with City finishing in fifth place in the First Division, ahead of Manchester United for the first time since 1978!

In the summer of 1991 I decided to celebrate my Irish roots with a visit to Dublin where "coincidentally" City were playing a friendly against local side Bohemians. I arrived late in the evening and booked a room in a dubious looking hotel off O'Connell Street and went straight into the bar for a few pints of the "black stuff". As I entered the room everybody seemed to turn around as the band immediately struck up with "Dirty Old Town". Time seemed to stand still. Here I was in search of my Irish roots and the band were playing a song about Salford. The following afternoon I walked up Grafton Street to go to O'Donoghues which was the pub where dad's favourites The Dubliners used to play. I had noticed that Jack Charlton's pub The Baggott was a little further along the road so I decided to slip in there, too. As I walked in I felt immediately disappointed to have left the bustling O'Donoghues as the bar was completely empty. That is apart from a tall ginger haired guy who was at the other end of the room to me and who seemed to be giving instructions to one or two young fellows about the position of amplifiers and drum kit. He seemed vaguely familiar. I ordered a pint, sat down on a bar stool and idly read the paper. Cables were plugged in around me and I looked at the barman and then at my watch. Five o'clock. This place is dead I decided and returned to my hotel for a wash and some tea. Two hours later I was in a taxi passing The Baggott only to see huge crowds queuing out of the door. As the evening wore on I gave it little thought but was horrified next day to read in the local paper that David Bowie had played an impromptu gig there with his new group the Tin Machine!

That summer mum's health started to fail. She had trouble breathing anyway due to having had emphysema for some twenty years. She regularly reminded us that this disease normally struck down coal miners and heavy smokers. She was neither of those, she laughed. But this was different as this was her heart that was causing her problems. At first she had to wear a monitor which was the size of an accordion and resembled a bus conductor's ticket machine. Then she was taken into North Manchester General Hospital or Crumpsall as it was known locally. Dad who was always the colossus of the family suddenly looked lost. I soon realised that it was not just a matter of visiting mum in hospital but also making sure that dad was OK. I bought him a ticket for the first home game of the season against Liverpool. It was the first game that he had seen live for years and as we walked together along Upper Lloyd Street South and turned into Claremont Road my mind went back to the late sixties and our first visits to Maine Road together. We would park our Austin 1100 in one of the many tiny terraced streets that surrounded the stadium, pay two shillings to the fastest West Indian teenager who asked us to "mind our car", and head off in the direction of the floodlights, my heart beating with joy and anticipation. I would hold dad's hand tightly and hang on to his every word as he pointed out groundsman Stan Gibson's house next to the Souvenir shop. Tonight it was difficult engaging dad in conversation. His mind was clearly elsewhere. In the hospital ward in Crumpsall which we had left earlier in the evening. As we entered the turnstiles I realised that it was I who was leading dad to our seats and pointing out things to him. The changing of the guard.

The game itself was exciting. City contained record signing Keith Curle as captain but it was David White who stole the headlines with two goals as the Blues romped home by two goals to one. Liverpool, who were now managed by Graeme Souness, were without the injured Ian Rush but still possessed a powerful midfield of Ronnie Whelan, Steve McMahon, Ray Houghton and a young Steve McManaman. Up front John Barnes was partnered by new signing Dean Saunders who had made a hero out of Niall Quinn back in April. The Blues held on for a famous victory on a hot August night and dad said that he had enjoyed the game as we made our way back to the car.

City continued their fine form as the season developed. A long trip down to Southampton in November was rewarded with a three goal victory with two goals from young Mike Sheron and one from big Niall. The Saints that day included a young Alan Shearer who revealed in the programme that his favourite music was that of Phil Collins. Enough said! Other highlights included a brilliant home victory by four goals over title bound Leeds United who had Eric Cantona in their side. It looked like this victory would hand the title over to United who were battling with Leeds at the top of the table. The following week I stood on the Stretford End with hundreds of very vocal Blues as ten man City secured a valuable point thanks to a Keith Curle penalty.

Match programmes hinted at just how little money City had at the time. Early in the season there was a photograph of the new blue seats which had been installed at the front of the North Stand. They could not afford to replace the seats in the top half of the stand which remained a vulgar shade of green! Another programme announced the "mickey mouse" reconstruction of the Platt Lane Stand with its "executive boxes" for those tempted by corporate hospitality. Its demolition gave me more cause to look back. This was the end of the ground from where I was introduced to the Blues back in October 1966 as Colin Bell, Mike Summerbee, Tony Book, Mike Doyle, Neil Young, Alan Oakes, and Glyn Pardoe were just beginning to find their feet in the First Division. Francis Lee was to join the club from Bolton a few weeks later and the rest, as they say, was history!

We could decide on the day of the game if we were going to the match, pay at the gate and devour every inch of the programme while listening to the brass band as kick off approached. City goalkeeper Harry Dowd wore a green shirt, black shorts and black socks as he put down his gloves in the back of the nets. The outfield players were numbered one to eleven on shirts which bore neither sponsors' logos nor players' names. Not even a club crest in 1966. Just sky blue and white. As the teams were announced dad would write down the changes including the name of the single substitute. There were invalid carriages in all four corners of the pitch and you could count the chimney pots on the houses above the tunnels in the corners of the Kippax. The open Scoreboard End a million miles away at the other end of the pitch contained the small square scoreboard from which you could check the half time scores using the A to Z in the programme. A Bovril or a Maxpax coffee at half time, before avoiding the puddles and horse manure in the Kippax car park as we made our way gingerly back to the car in the semi darkness on the way home. I waited in huge anticipation every Saturday night outside the newsagent for The "Pink" to arrive. The familiar yellow van rounded the corner and the heroic driver leapt out clutching his valuable bundle tightly before depositing it onto the counter to the relief of a packed shop. As we surged forward copies were handed out over my head to those who had already paid. Saturday night television with Doctor Who and Val Doonican passed me by as I read the print off the "Pink" and the City programme while waiting for the signature tune which announced Match of the Day with David Coleman and Jimmy Hill. It was absolutely nail-biting as we waited to see who would be the featured game.

The new season heralded the beginning of the Premier League. Sky television, for those who could afford it, chose City against Q.P.R. to be its first live televised game on a Monday night. The fanfare included dancing girls, a live band, fireworks, and even a parachute drop. The ground was covered with T.V. cables and microphones. There were cameras covering every possible angle. I was sat in a new seat in the main stand just to the left of the tunnel, and as the teams took to the field Macker turned to me and remarked "What was all that about? Just who are they trying to impress?" I did not reply. After all, long before any of the new "razzmatazz", this was our City.